WHY SHOULD I GO TO DUBLIN

WHY SHOULD I GO TO ↙
DUBLIN

THE CITY YOU DEFINITELY NEED TO
VISIT BEFORE YOU TURN 30 (OR 130)

THIS IS WHY!

Dublin is a truly diverse city. Steeped in history – from its Viking roots to the lasting impact of the Irish Rebellion – the city's past has shaped its rich and vibrant culture. It's buzzing with creative energy and proudly holds its status as a UNESCO City of Literature.

A welcoming pub is never far away, but its food scene is also a highlight. In recent years, the city has been booming with new and trendy restaurants and bars, while you can still count on finding a hearty Irish stew or the perfect pint of Guinness. There are plenty of vintage shops and unique boutiques. And best of all, Dublin is dotted with city parks and is surrounded by amazing nature. From beaches and cliffs to mountains and meadows, it offers the perfect mix of urban life and rural escape.

Dublin isn't the cheapest destination, but travelling there doesn't have to break the bank. The city is compact and easy to get around, so walk, cycle, or use public transport rather than taking expensive taxis. Book affordable accommodation, explore the parks, dive into the sea, go for a hike, and make the most of Dublin's many free museums. You'll also find fantastic meals at fair prices if you know where to look.

Whether you're a foodie, a history buff, a bookworm, a nature-lover, or a barfly, Dublin is your city! Most of all, it's the people who make Dublin unforgettable. The Irish are famously warm and welcoming, always happy to stop for a chat. One thing is certain: once you've been, you'll want to go back for more.

CONTENTS

NEIGHBOURHOODS 8
PRACTICAL INFO 12

WHEN TO TRAVEL 30
LIFE IN DUBLIN 40

FOOD AND DRINKS 106
GOING OUT 130

GREEN DUBLIN 170
OUTSIDE OF DUBLIN 184

SHOPPING 142

Index 188
Who made this book? 191-192

NEIGHBOURHOODS

GLASNEVIN (DUBLIN 9)

DRUMCONDRA (DUBLIN 9)

SMITHFIELD (DUBLIN 7)

NORTH CITY (DUBLIN 1)

TEMPLE BAR (DUBLIN 2)

THE LIBERTIES & PORTOBELLO (DUBLIN 8)

CITY CENTRE (DUBLIN 2)

RANELAGH (DUBLIN 6)

RATHMINES (DUBLIN 6)

Dublin is divided into 22 numbered districts, indicated by their postcodes. The River Liffey separates the city into north and south, with even numbers indicating the south side and odd the north. Generally, the higher a district number, the further it is from the city centre. This chapter highlights the districts with the most to see and do. Some are just minutes from the city centre, while others lie further out, but all are well worth a visit.

SOUTH

City Centre & Temple Bar (Dublin 2)

Home to Dublin's main attractions – Dublin Castle, St. Stephen's Green, The Temple Bar pub, Trinity College, and the hip and happening Camden Street. Dublin 2 attracts tourists and students alike.

Ballsbridge & Sandymount (Dublin 4)

A leafy, green area, housing Dublin's embassies, Aviva Stadium, Herbert Park, and the wide coastal stretch of Sandymount Strand.

Ranelagh & Rathmines (Dublin 6)

Rathmines is a lively hub for students and young professionals, while Ranelagh charms with its red-brick townhouses and green streets. Both feature numerous lovely neighbourhood shops, pubs, and restaurants.

The Liberties & Portobello (Dublin 8)

This area blends creativity and history, with art galleries, whiskey distilleries, and the Guinness Storehouse alongside St. Patrick's Cathedral and Christ Church. It's also a residential neighbourhood with Georgian townhouses and great brunch spots.

Blackrock (County Dublin)

A vibrant seaside town with cafés, restaurants, boutiques, and the beloved Blackrock market. Plus Seapoint, a great spot for a swim.

Dún Laoghaire (County Dublin)

A popular seaside resort in Victorian times, Dún Laoghaire is still a great place to go sailing and swimming. Or visit the local market and walk along the harbour.

NORTH

North City (Dublin 1)

This busy area in the heart of the city is home to the Four Courts, the Spire, and Hugh Lane Gallery. You can also find a shopping area, with chain stores as well as department store Arnott's at Dublin 1.

Clontarf (Dublin 3)

A peaceful coastal suburb with scenic spots like Bull Island, Dollymount Strand, and the large St. Anne's Park.

Smithfield (Dublin 7)

An up-and-coming area where Victorian terraces meet modern apartment blocks, known for the iconic Jameson Distillery tower and the indie favourite Lighthouse Cinema.

Glasnevin & Drumcondra (Dublin 9)

This area offers a mix of nature, history, and sports, with highlights like the National Botanic Gardens, Glasnevin Cemetery, and Croke Park stadium. Drumcondra, home to a university, is known for its affordable bars and restaurants.

Howth (Dublin 13)

Just 25 minutes from the city centre by train, Howth offers fresh seafood by the harbour and beautiful cliff walks with sweeping ocean views.

TRAVEL

Airport transfers

Dublin's international airport is found seven kilometres north of the city. You can travel into the city by bus or taxi. If you're travelling alone or as a pair, the bus is the most affordable option. However, if you're in a group of three or more, taking a taxi might be cheaper and more convenient. There are several bus operators that will bring you to Dublin city and the greater Dublin area. Check which bus route works best for you and prebook your ticket on *dublinairport.com/to-from-the-airport/by bus*. Some operators allow you to purchase a ticket on board, but it's best to confirm this in advance.

Travelling by ferry

For a more spectacular way to arrive in Dublin that will allow you to bring your own car, taking the ferry is an ideal choice. Dublin Port offers regular ferry connections with England, Wales, and even France. Conveniently located near the city centre, the port provides easy access to town by taxi, bus, or tram (Luas).

Public transport

Dublin has a reliable public transport system with various options for getting around the city. You can either take a green-and-yellow double-decker bus (TFI), the Luas tram, or – if you want to visit the surrounding areas – the DART, Dublin's coastal train. The best way to never miss a bus, tram or train is to download the free Transport for Ireland *TFI Live* app.

The bus generally operates between 5.30am and 11.30pm. However, some routes run 24 hours. The tram, called Luas, connects the city centre with Dublin's suburbs. There are two lines: the Green Line, which runs from north to south, and the Red Line, which runs from east to west.

The DART has several stations in central Dublin and runs along the coast. It's a great way to explore the beautiful coastline near Dublin, with access to great hiking (and cycling) spots like Howth in the north and Greystones in the south. It's good to know that bicycles are allowed on board during off-peak travel times.

The easiest and cheapest way to travel is by using the TFI Leap Card. This can be used on buses, trams, and trains – and even for renting a Dublin Bike. You

TRAVEL

can purchase the Leap Card at many PostPoints and all post offices. Young adults (aged 19-25) and Dublin based students can hop around Dublin for just €1 per ride with a Leap Card, but Young Adult and Student Leap Cards must be ordered online. You can easily top-up your card with Travel Credit and/or Tickets. For more information, check out *leapcard.ie*. Contactless payment is not yet available on public transport.

On buses or trains, you just touch in as you enter, but on the Luas, you must also touch out as you exit.

Cycling

Why not explore Dublin by bike? Dublin Bikes, the city's shared bike system, is easy to use and available at over a hundred stations throughout the city. You'll need to register for an account online (*dublinbikes.ie*) or through the *Dublin Bikes* app. Once registered, you'll receive a code that unlocks bikes at the stations. There are several plans available, from 1-day and 3-day passes to an annual subscription. The first 30 minutes of each ride are free, after that, charges apply based on the duration of your journey. Just be extra cautious if you are not used to cycling on the left side of the road. Whenever possible, use dedicated cycling routes for a safer and more comfortable ride.

Taxis

You can either hail a taxi or use one of the taxi apps. Just make sure the car has an official taxi sign, as there are unlicensed taxis driving around. Taxi drivers in Dublin are known for being very friendly and they are always up for a good chat.

WHERE TO STAY

Places to stay in Dublin are generally 'at the higher end of affordable', as in any of the more expensive European cities. That means either saving up or booking a hostel. And even then, don't necessarily count on stylish or trendy accommodation. However, it does help to visit Dublin off-season, and sometimes you can find good last-minute deals.

Dublin 2 and the south side of the city are where much of the action happens – most pubs, restaurants, and cultural highlights can be found there. While accommodation there can be a bit pricier, you're right in the heart of the action. That said, there are also good options in other neighbourhoods, such as Dublin 1, which is just across the river and close to the city centre.

HOSTELS

Abbey Court Hostel

29 Bachelors Walk, North City, Dublin 1, abbey-court.com

Abbey Court has been a fixture in the Dublin hostel scene for over 25 years. As it's not a chain, but family-run instead, a personal experience is guaranteed. As is the cheapest pint of Guinness in Dublin.

Clink I Lár

35-36 Abbey Street Upper, North City, Dublin 1, clinkhostels.com/dublin

Pink, orange, light blue, yellow: the ambience at Clink I Lár is as colourful as the cocktails in its bar. The built-in box beds make for a cosy experience, even in the dorm rooms.

Latroupe Jacobs Inn

21-28 Talbot Place, Mountjoy, Dublin 1, latroupe.com/en/latroupe-jacobs-inn/hostel

The look and feel of a hotel with the vibes of a hostel; look no further if you're looking for the best of both worlds. Its bar, known for creative cocktails and good quality beers, attracts locals and visitors alike.

Ashfield Hostel

19-20 D'Olier Street, City Centre, Dublin 2, ashfieldhostel.com

It doesn't get much more central than this. Ashfield offers private rooms, eighteen-bed mixed dorms, and everything in between.

The Dawson Hostel

35 Dawson Street, City Centre, Dublin 2, thedawsonhostel.ie

The Dawson claims to be your key to Dublin. Given its central location, you will indeed find much of what this city has to offer not far from its front door. Having St. Stephen's Green a stone's throw away is another asset.

Abigail's Hostel

7-9 Aston Quay, Temple Bar, Dublin 2, abigailshostel.com

Abigail's ranks among the top hostels in Dublin and beyond, overlooks the river Liffey, and provides a fully equipped kitchen. What is not to like?

Generator Dublin

Smithfield Square, Smithfield, Dublin 7, generator.com/hostels/dublin

A very hip hostel in the Smithfield neighbourhood. With events every night, a lot is going on, but should you want to leave the premises, Jameson Distillery is next door, and the beating heart of Dublin is not far away.

HOTELS

Temple Bar Inn

40-47 Fleet Street,
Temple Bar, Dublin 2,
templebarinn.com

If you want to be in the middle of everything, and enjoy a nearby swimming pool with a great discount, this is your hotel. Unfortunately, the Temple Bar Inn doesn't come cheap.

The Ferryman Townhouse

35 Sir John Rogerson's
Quay, Docklands, Dublin 2,
theferrymantownhouse.ie

The pub is traditionally Irish, the fifteen rooms above it stylish, yet affordable. After a nightcap in one of its three bars, frequented by locals, it's an easy 'commute' to your room.

Blackrock B&B

16 Booterstown Avenue,
Blackrock, County Dublin,
blackrock-bb.hotel-
inn-dublin.com

While it's not right in the city centre, this charming two-room B&B is nestled in the seaside village of Blackrock, known for lovely restaurants and shops, and the popular swimming spot Seapoint. With Booterstown DART and bus station just around the corner, getting into the heart of Dublin is quick and easy.

Ariel House

50-54 Lansdowne Road,
Ballsbridge, Dublin 4,
arielhouse.ie

Housed in three elegant Victorian townhouses dating back to 1850, once home to a wealthy shipping merchant and his family. Ariel House combines historical charm with a touch of luxury, though that luxury comes at a price.

↓ GENERATOR DUBLIN

Maples House Hotel

*79-81 Iona Road,
Glasnevin, Dublin 9,
mapleshousehotel.ie*

From its red-brick residential appearance to its homey decorations and wallpaper, this family-run hotel in the northern part of Dublin does have every intention of making you feel right at home. Even the room prices are welcoming.

GOOD TO KNOW

Money

The currency used in Dublin and the Republic of Ireland is the euro. Credit and debit cards are widely accepted, and contactless payment is commonly used. Dublin is not the most budget-friendly city to visit. It ranks among the top ten most expensive cities to stay in across Europe, but there are still plenty of budget-friendly options for eating out and accommodation.

Charging

It's a good idea to bring a travel adapter, as Ireland uses a 230-volt power supply and a type G plug, which features three rectangular pins.

Walking around

The best way to explore Dublin is on foot, as it's a relatively compact city. Many restaurants, shops, and attractions are located in the city centre within easy walking distance of one another. In fact, walking is often quicker than taking the bus, especially given the frequent traffic congestion.

Language

As soon as you arrive in Dublin, you'll notice that all the signs are in both English and Irish (Gaelic). This is quite remarkable, given that only a small percentage of the Irish population still speaks Gaelic as a first language. English, as the primary language, will easily get you around anywhere.

Weather

Dublin has a temperate climate, with summer temperatures rarely exceeding 23°C and generally mild winters. However, the weather can be quite unpredictable, so always pack some warm clothes, even in summer. An umbrella might also come in handy. You might think Dubliners spend most of their time indoors because of the weather, but don't worry, whenever the sun comes out, so do the locals!

Look left, look right

Traffic in Ireland drives on the left side of the road, so be cautious when crossing the street if you're not used to it. Thankfully, most pedestrian crossings are clearly marked with instructions on which way to look.

Museums

One of the best things about Dublin is that most major cultural institutions are free to visit. The National Museum of Ireland, The Irish Museum of Modern Art (IMMA), Hugh Lane Gallery, The Photo Museum Ireland, and many others welcome visitors free of charge.

Dublin pass

If you're planning to visit Dublin's top tourist attractions and want to explore the city with a hop-on, hop-off bus tour, the Dublin Pass might be a good option. It can save you up to 50 per cent compared to buying individual tickets, depending on how many attractions you decide to visit. Check out *dublincitypass.com* for more information.

Restaurants

Dubliners love to brunch, lunch, or dine out and it's best to make a reservation if you want to be sure to have a table. Many restaurants have 'early bird' offers; discounted meals, especially for dinner if you arrive

Guinness
DARKEY KELLY'S

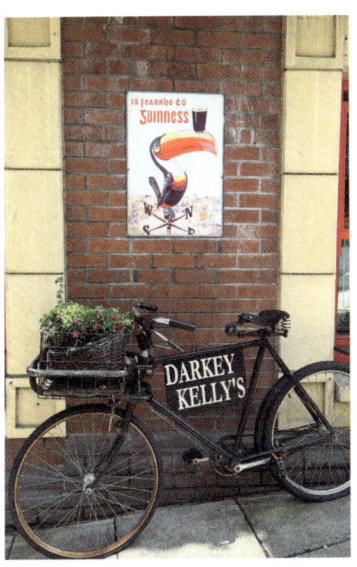

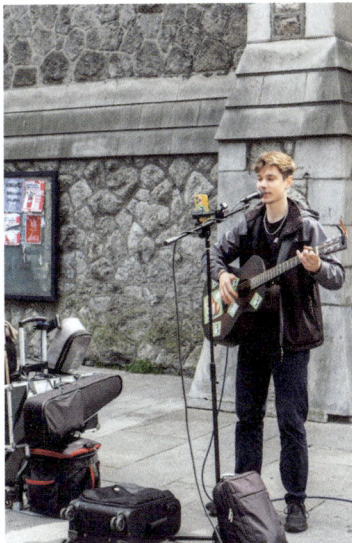

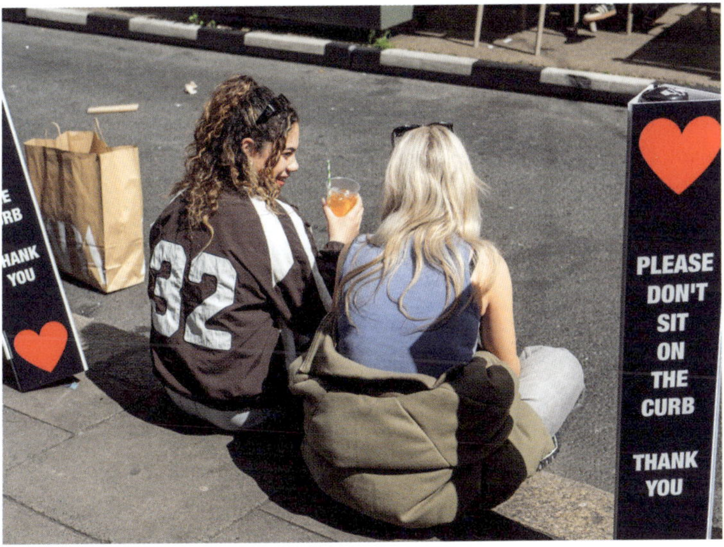
PLEASE DON'T SIT ON THE CURB
THANK YOU

before a specific time. Tipping varies by venue, but around 10% is standard. However, many restaurants include a service charge in the bill, which covers service and is shared among the staff. In this case, tipping is not necessary but of course appreciated.

Food

The Irish love their traditional dishes: hearty Irish stew, full Irish breakfast, and classic fish and chips are still popular staples. These traditional meals are most often found in pubs. Of course, modern and international cuisine is also widely available throughout town. Chefs across Ireland take pride in using local ingredients, from fresh seafood and high-quality dairy to succulent lamb, flavourful sausages, oats, and a variety of Irish cheeses. With such a rich culinary landscape, Ireland has plenty to offer.

Nightlife

The official drinking age in Ireland is 18, but many clubs in Dublin have a minimum age of 21, and sometimes even 25, so be sure to check in advance. Dublin has a vibrant nightlife scene, with many pubs open seven days a week. You'll find locals having drinks both after work and after dinner (which is usually around 8pm). Pubs and clubs close relatively early due to licensing laws, typically around 2.30am.

Shopping

The best place for shopping is south of the River Liffey, which runs through the centre of Dublin. There you'll discover a wide variety of interesting shops, from independent boutiques and vintage shops in Temple Bar to bookshops, home décor stores, Irish design shops, and high-end retailers in and around Grafton and Henry Street. On the north side of the river, you'll mostly find large chain stores. There are some smaller, charming shops in neighbourhoods like Ranelagh, the Liberties, and Rathmines. The surrounding villages of Dublin, like Sandymount, Blackrock, and Monkstown also offer a selection of quaint little shops.

Hiking & Cycling

Dublin is renowned for its stunning surroundings, including beaches, parks, and mountains. No visit to the city is complete without exploring these beautiful green landscapes. Hike the scenic Howth Cliff Walk north of Dublin or climb to the summit of Killiney Hill for breathtaking views. For a more relaxed experience, go cycling through Phoenix Park, which has plenty of trails. And if you're feeling adventurous, try mountain biking in the Wicklow Mountains. Most of the green surroundings are easily accessible by public transport.

Swimming

One of Dublin's main attractions is its location on Dublin Bay, along the Irish Sea. A short ride by bus or DART train will quickly take you to the coast. Although the sea can be icy cold, the Irish are known for taking dips year-round. Seapoint, Vico Baths, Bull Island, and the Forty Foot are popular spots for a swim nearby. The official bathing season runs from 1st June to 15th September, during which the water quality is regularly monitored by the Dublin Council. Due to occasional pollution, swimming is sometimes prohibited. For the latest updates, visit *beaches.ie*.

DUBLIN IN SPRING

Daffodils, cherry blossom, roses ... spring is the most colourful time to visit Dublin. Take a stroll through parks like St. Stephen's Green or Merrion Square to soak up their spring beauty. Leafy neighbourhoods, like Portobello, Ranelagh, and Ballsbridge are worth a visit too. Spring is also one of the best times to hike along the coast or in the mountains.

One of Dublin's biggest and most famous festivals, St. Patrick's Festival, takes place in spring. Ireland's patron saint is honoured with parades, live performances, markets, and lively pub celebrations. Every year from 15th-17th March, this festival takes over the entire city. St. Patrick's Day is celebrated in many parts of the world, but Dublin is by far the best place to party.

In May, Merrion Square comes alive with the International Literature Festival, a ten-day celebration of books and storytelling. Also in May, dance lovers can catch the Dublin Dance Festival, showcasing contemporary performances from around the world. On 16th June, the city celebrates Bloomsday, a literary tribute to Leopold Bloom, the fictional protagonist of James Joyce's *Ulysses*, Dublin's most celebrated novel.

If you're feeling brave, join the locals and dive into the icy waters of the Irish Sea. There are plenty of designated spots where swimming is allowed. The best time for a dip is on a warmer, sunny spring day in May or June, as sea temperatures remain quite low – between 10°C and 13°C.

DUBLIN IN SUMMER

First off, pack some swimwear! A plunge in the chilly Dublin Bay is a must and an unforgettable part of the Dublin summer experience.

While Dublin summers may not be as hot as elsewhere, locals make the most of any sunny spell. You'll find people strolling or picnicking in parks, outdoor festivals popping up all over the city, street feasts in various neighbourhoods, and crowds spilling out of pubs, enjoying drinks and chats in the open air. It's also the perfect time of year to enjoy outdoor live music and open-air cinema screenings.

Keep in mind, summer is also the busiest season, with lots of tourists in town, which means hostels and hotels tend to be more expensive. Still, it's one of the most enjoyable times to be in Dublin. Love some good music and partying? Then you've got to check out Longitude in Marlay Park in July, Dublin's top outdoor festival for pop and hip hop. In August, Herbert Park offers the perfect mix of music, food, and fun during the Big Grill festival.

Summer is also a great time to explore Dublin's outdoor markets. Irish Village Markets pop up across the city, offering incredible food stalls. On Sundays, the Herbert Park Farmers Market is perfect for picking up local treats and enjoying a laid-back picnic. And if you're up for a little adventure, hop on the DART to charming seaside towns like Dún Laoghaire or Blackrock for more great markets and a scenic stroll along the coast.

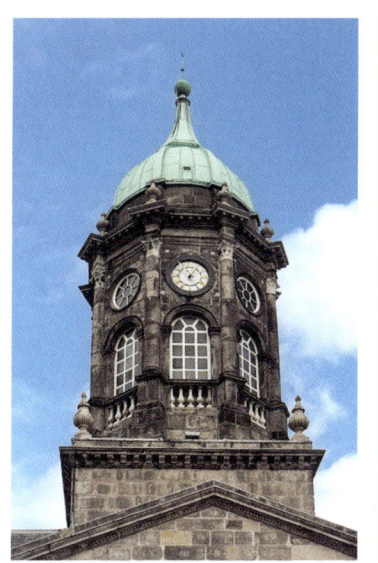

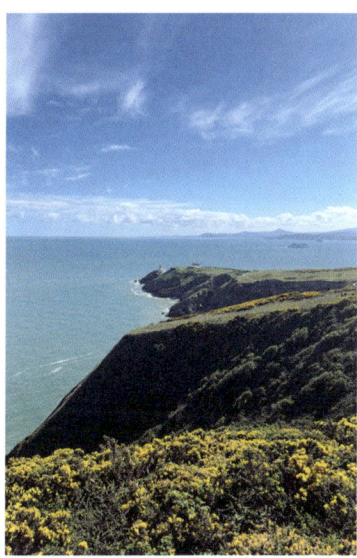

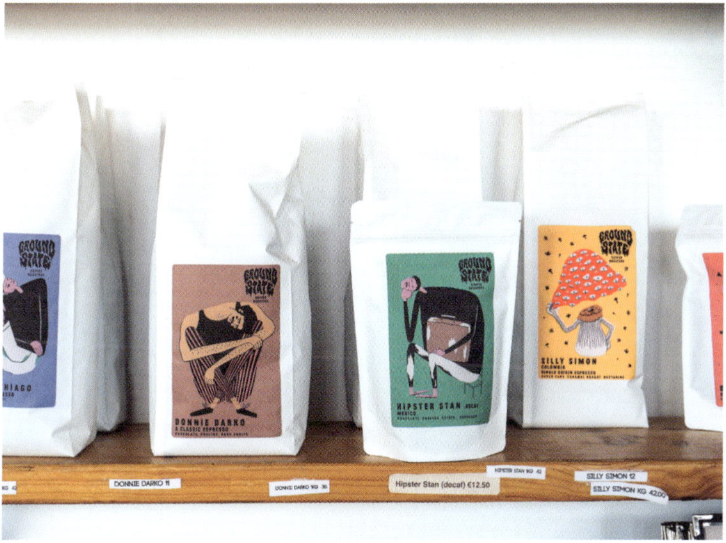
GROUND STATE
DONNIE DARKO
A CLASSIC ESPRESSO
GROUND STATE
HIPSTER STAN DECAF
MEXICO
GROUND STATE
SILLY SIMON
COLOMBIA
SINGLE ORIGIN ESPRESSO
DONNIE DARKO 11
DONNIE DARKO KG 36
Hipster Stan (decaf) €12.50
HIPSTER STAN KG 42
SILLY SIMON 12
SILLY SIMON KG 42.00

DUBLIN IN AUTUMN

As the days become shorter, Dublin's parks come alive with autumn colours, and the pubs feel even cosier. Sure, it can get chilly and there might be a few rain showers, but there's no shortage of great indoor activities to enjoy. And what better way to warm up than with a pint of Guinness in one of the city's atmospheric pubs, like The Stag's Head, The Palace Bar, or O'Donoghue's?

Dublin is anything but boring in autumn. September kicks off the season with major cultural events like the Fringe Festival, Ireland's largest multidisciplinary arts festival, and the Dublin Theatre Festival. Or lose yourself in one of the many museums with free admission. The National Gallery of Ireland, with its three spacious floors, is particularly worth visiting. You could easily spend hours exploring its collection.

Rooted in ancient Celtic traditions, Halloween is celebrated in a big way in Dublin. People wear spooky fancy dress and there are pub crawls all over town. Around this time, the darkest festival of the year, the Bram Stoker Festival, also takes place. It is named after the Dublin-born author who created *Dracula*. The festival spans four days and nights, filled with all sorts of gothic and supernatural experiences.

It's also the perfect time of year to take the *Dead Interesting Tour* at Glasnevin Cemetery. After all that ghostly excitement, head next door for a pint at the adjoining John Kavanagh's Pub, better known as The Gravediggers.

DUBLIN IN WINTER

Thanks to Dublin's temperate climate, winters are rarely very cold. They can be a bit wet, but with so much happening around the city, it's easy to forget about the rain. Christmas is celebrated in great abundance, with festive lights all over town. To truly get in the mood, head to the Christmas Market at Dublin Castle. There is also the Dublin Winter Light festival with artistic light projections on iconic buildings, bridges, statues, and more.

One of the best ways to warm up is by booking a whiskey tour with a tasting. Try the Jameson Distillery or the beautifully designed Roe & Co Distillery. If whiskey's not your favourite drink, head to the Guinness Storehouse, where you can learn all about Ireland's famous black beer. You'll also find plenty of winter spirit in Dublin's pubs. Many serve hearty, warming dishes like Irish stew, colcannon, and shepherd's pie: perfect comfort food. And with many live gigs, there's no better place to be on a chilly day.

New Year's Festival Dublin is a big deal. For three days, the streets come alive with live music, light shows, and non-stop parties. The countdown itself is also pretty spectacular, and if you're by the coast, villages along Dublin Bay, like Howth and Dún Laoghaire, also put on impressive firework displays.

The festivities don't stop there. January brings TradFest, a celebration of traditional Irish music. In February, the Dublin International Film Festival takes over the city for eleven days, screening the best of international and Irish cinema in venues all around town.

HISTORY

Tale of two origins

The first settlement in what we now call the Dublin Bay area was reported almost 2,000 years ago. However, references to its current name (Dublin in English, Áth Cliath in Irish) date back to 841 CE and 1368 CE respectively. The Vikings settled in the 9th century near the mouth of the river Liffey and called it Dyflin after the Irish word for black pool, Duiblinn or Dubh Linn. Around the same time, the Celts created a small village a little further upstream, but its name, Áth Cliath, wasn't recorded until 1368.

The Anglo-Norman invasion

The first real growth of the city took place after Henry II, King of England, invaded Ireland in 1169. He made Dublin its military and judicial centre and immigrants from England and mainland Europe flocked to the city. Over time, the Catholic city was dominated and then suppressed by a Protestant minority. Dublin's Catholic churches and monasteries were confiscated, one of which was transformed into Trinity College in 1592.

Doors of Dublin

Further British domination was the consequence of the 1800 Act of Union and the rise of the United Kingdom of Great Britain and Ireland. Dublin's parliament was dissolved, and under British rule, Dublin transformed from a medieval city into the city that we know now. Large Georgian streets and squares were created, and Georgian buildings were erected. In accordance with the architectural fashion at the time, planning regulations were strict, harmony prevailed, and decorative elements were limited. One of the only ways to distinguish oneself from the neighbours was to paint the front door in a bright colour. To this day, many Dubliners do.

The Potato Famine

In the middle of the 19th century, the Irish depended heavily on potatoes for nutrition, so when the potato crops were infected by a plague, famine struck between 1847 and 1852. Millions died or fled the country, and its population declined by twenty-five per cent. Dublin was least affected; thanks to its port and trading networks, food remained more or less available, especially for those who could afford the hiked prices.

Beer, biscuits, whiskey

After the famine, Dublin's decline set in, and it lost the industrialisation battle to Belfast. The population grew poorer as unemployment rose. The many unskilled workers found their main employers in Guinness Brewery, Jameson Distillery, and Jacob's Biscuit Factory. Consequently, new working-class neighbourhoods rose around those sites.

The Lockout

This class of low-skilled workers, with their low wages and long hours, provided fertile ground for the rise of trade unions, with the largest founded by James Larkin and James Connolly. To break the power of unions, in 1931, employers agreed to fire any worker that joined the unions' ranks, an act that became known as the Lockout. Violent riots and bitter clashes between unionists and the

police emerged. To defend the strikers, Larkin and Connolly created the Irish Citizen Army, which developed into a paramilitary organisation. After six months of strikes and demonstrations, hunger and starvation became so prevalent among the workers' families that most decided to leave the union and go back to work. This period left a mark on Dublin and its history, and statues and references to Larkin and Connolly can still be found throughout the city.

Road to independence

The Irish will to cut loose from Britain grew in the early 1900s. During the 1916 Easter Rising, thousands of Irish Republicans were arrested and their leaders executed. Three years later, the volunteer Irish Republican Army (IRA) rebelled against British rule for three years, seriously damaging Dublin in the process. It took a Civil War and another year to gain some form of independence from the Brits when in 1922, the so-called Irish Free State was created as a dominion of the British Commonwealth. For many Irish that wasn't enough. After fifteen years of internal conflicts, a new state was created in 1937, called Ireland (or Éire in Irish). Although Dublin had been surpassed by Belfast as the largest and most industrialised city on the island, Dublin remained the capital. Northern Ireland, and Belfast with it, had decided to remain part of the United Kingdom.

Four Bloody Sundays

Of the four Bloody Sundays the Irish have experienced, two took place in Dublin in the early 20th century. The first, in 1913, stemmed from a violent and eventually deadly crackdown of a trade union gathering led by Jim Larkin. The second happened during the War of Independence in November 1920. An IRA Dublin Brigade led by Michael Collins assassinated British spies, after which British troops raided a football match, killing fourteen people. The third was in Belfast, when sixteen were killed in violent clashes between Irish Catholics and Protestant loyalists. Famous from the U2 song, the last of four Bloody Sundays happened on 30th January 1972, when the British Army opened fire at demonstrators in Derry, Northern Ireland, killing thirteen people. This Bloody Sunday left its mark on Dublin when protesters destroyed the British Embassy in Merrion Square two days later.

Irish culture

As part of its nationalist movement, ancient Gaelic traditions experienced a revival throughout the 20th century. This included renewed interest in its mythology and legends rooted in prehistoric times, passed down orally, and adapted to Christian norms and values. Also, Irish dance and Irish folk music became popular again. Stepdance, in which the dancers keep their upper bodies stiff and move their feet in complex rhythms, supposedly dates to ancient Celtic times. It was promoted again in the 1920s and is still practiced on a large scale today. Famous bands like the Dubliners included Irish folk elements in their music.

Modern Dublin

Dublin remained a relatively poor city throughout much of the 20th century, and the city centre was dotted with working-class tenements. Alternative housing for the working class was only very gradually made available, and these tenements weren't taken down until the 1960s. After joining the European

Community in 1973, Ireland started to evolve, although slowly at first. But in the 1990s, the economy grew so fast that Dublin experienced a building boom, which lasted until the financial crash of 2008 hit Ireland hard.

Silicon Dock

With a little help from the IMF and the EU, and thanks to its thriving financial and tech sectors, Ireland regained its economic footing. This is most visible in Dublin's Grand Canal area, which has experienced a total makeover and is now bustling with big tech companies and high-tech start-ups. The trend started with the arrival of Google in 2004. Its location between the U.S. and Europe, the English language, and the attractive fiscal climate all contributed to Dublin's popularity as a tech hub. The likes of Meta and X quickly followed suit and established their European headquarters in the same area, dubbing it 'Silicon Docks'. The influx of high-tech knowledge workers that followed contributed to Dublin becoming one of the most expensive cities in Europe.

New migration

Over much of the 19th and 20th century, Dublin mainly saw people arriving from different parts of the country, looking for jobs and a better future, and from England, sent there to govern and police its overseas territory. It also saw many of its inhabitants leave the city in an attempt to escape poverty and hunger. That has all changed. The economic booms in the 1990s and of late inspired people of Irish descent to return, but also attracted new migrants, mainly from India, Brazil, and Eastern and Central Europe. More and more languages are spoken in the streets of Dublin, and many international restaurants and shops have been founded.

City of Literature

Storytelling is rooted in Irish culture. Before novels filled bookshelves, stories were passed down through generations by word of mouth. In medieval times, Irish Christian monks began writing these stories down in beautiful, intricate manuscripts.

The centuries of conflicts, oppressions and political struggles in Ireland gave the people plenty to talk and write about. Pubs played a big role in this. These weren't just there to have a pint; they became gathering places for writers, artists, and intellectuals to share ideas and debate the goings-on in the world. As a result, Ireland has produced many brilliant writers, poets, and playwrights, such as Oscar Wilde, James Joyce, and Samuel Beckett, to name a few. In 2010, Dublin was designated a UNESCO City of Literature.

SIGHTSEEING

Georgian squares

Built in the 18th and early 19th centuries, Dublin's Georgian squares are an iconic part of the city's architecture and history. Lined with red-brick façades and colourful doors, and beautiful parks at their centres, these squares are some of the finest examples of Dublin's classic Georgian architecture. You can find five of these around the city: Merrion Square, Fitzwilliam Square, St. Stephen's Green, Mountjoy Square, and Parnell Square.

The Garden of Remembrance

Parnell Square East, North City, Dublin 1, heritageireland.ie/ places-to-visit/garden- of-remembrance

Opened on the 50th anniversary of the 1916 Easter Rising, the Garden of Remembrance is a peaceful memorial in the heart of Dublin, dedicated to those who died in the struggle for Irish independence. Its cross-shaped pool, designed by Dáithí Hanly, features mosaics of broken weapons, symbolising the end of battle. The striking *Children of Lir* sculpture, in which four children are transformed into swans and will remain so for 900 years before becoming human again, represents transformation. In 2011, Queen Elizabeth II laid a wreath at this memorial, marking a historic moment in Irish-British relations.

Dublin Castle

Dame Street, City Centre, Dublin 2, dublincastle.ie

Originally the site of a Viking settlement, Dublin Castle was constructed in the early 13th century and served as the headquarters of English, and later British, rule in Ireland for centuries. Following Ireland's Independence in 1922, the castle was handed over to the new Irish government. It has since become a popular tourist attraction. Daily guided tours and audio guides give rich insights into the building's key historical events and features. If you're there on a sunny day, make sure to visit the peaceful Castle Gardens, located close to the original black pool that gave Dublin its name.

The National Library of Ireland

7-8 Kildare Street, City Centre, Dublin 2, nli.ie

Founded in 1877, the National Library of Ireland now holds over 12 million Irish and Irish-related items, from books, maps, and newspapers to music and photographs. Since 1890, it has been housed in its current building, known for its stunning domed Reading Room. Visitors can explore the collections and exhibitions, including the award-winning W.B. Yeats exhibition, free of charge.

Old Library of Trinity College Dublin

College Green, South-East Inner City, Dublin 2, visittrinity.ie

Located on the campus of Trinity College, the Old Library is part of Ireland's largest copyright library, which contains over 4.5 million books, maps, manuscripts, and musical works. Since 1661, it has been home to the Book of Kells, a world-famous illuminated manuscript made by Celtic monks. The library also houses the Brian

Boru harp, Ireland's national symbol, and a copy of the 1916 Proclamation of the Irish Republic. You can book a ticket to see the Book of Kells and the Old Library, or go for the full Book of Kells Experience, which includes a spectacular digital exhibition.

The Four Courts

Inns Quay, Smithfield, Dublin 7, courts.ie/four-courts

Ireland's principal court building, the Four Courts, are home to the Supreme Court, Court of Appeal, High Court, and Dublin Circuit Court. Construction began in 1776, based on designs by Thomas Colley, and later additions were made by James Gandon. Though partially destroyed during the Civil War in 1922, it was restored and reopened in 1932. Today, the courts are still operational, and many courtrooms are open to the public.

Saint Patrick's Cathedral

St. Patrick's Close, The Liberties, Dublin 8, stpatrickscathedral.ie

St. Patrick's Cathedral, the national cathedral of the Church of Ireland, is one of few remaining buildings from medieval Dublin. It was founded in 1191 CE in honour of Saint Patrick, Ireland's patron saint, who is said to have baptised converts on this site 1,500 years ago. Visits to the cathedral are ticketed. There are daily guided tours and an app for self-guided visits. There is a lovely park in front of the cathedral, with great views of the building and its 100-metre-tall tower. It's a popular spot among Dubliners who come here to relax, take a stroll, or walk their dog.

Christ Church Cathedral

Christchurch Place, The Liberties, Dublin 8, christchurchcathedral.ie

The second of Dublin's two medieval cathedrals, Christ Church was founded by Sitric, Norse king of Dublin in 1030 CE, making it the oldest building in the city. Originally a Viking church, it has welcomed pilgrims and visitors for almost 1,000 years. The cathedral is home to a 12th-century crypt, one of the oldest and largest in Ireland and Britain. It contains fascinating artefacts and memorials and can still be visited today. To visit the cathedral, you can get a self-guided tour admission ticket.

National Botanic Gardens

Glasnevin, Dublin 9, botanicgardens.ie

Located in Glasnevin, the National Botanic Gardens is a scientific institution, containing more than 15,000 plant species and cultivars from around the world. Spread across a large site, the gardens' features include a rose garden, an alpine yard, a pond, a rock garden and an arboretum, but they are most famous for their beautifully restored historic glasshouses. Admission is free, and free guided tours are offered on Sundays.

MUSEUMS

EPIC – The Irish Emigration Museum

CHQ, Custom House Quay, North City, Dublin 1, epicchq.com

At this popular interactive museum, you can dive into Ireland's emigration history and learn about the 10 million Irish people who left their country and how they influenced the world. From music and dance to art, literature, and politics. Do you have Irish roots? At the Power of a Name exhibition, you can honour your heritage by adding your emigrant ancestor's name to the Legacy Wall.

14 Henrietta Street

14 Henrietta Street, North City, Dublin 1, 14henriettastreet.ie

This Georgian townhouse in North Dublin is filled with history. Built in the 1720s by a wealthy family with rooms for the masters, their children, and the servants, it looked very different at the time. Everything changed in the early 20th century when the need for cheap housing grew, and 14 Henrietta Street became a typical tenement home, packed with no fewer than a hundred tenants. The fascinating story of this house reflects the story of Dublin itself. You can only visit on a guided tour, so it's best to book your tickets in advance.

Hugh Lane Gallery

Charlemont House, Parnell Square North, North City, Dublin 1, hughlane.ie

A true mecca for Francis Bacon fans! This is where you can see his famously chaotic studio, preserved as if he had just walked out yesterday. His entire workspace was moved from London to Dublin, right down to the walls, ceiling, and even the staircase. But there's more to explore at this lovely museum, such as the Sean Scully Room and the magical Stained Glass Room featuring works by Harry Clarke. If you're into modern and contemporary art, Hugh Lane Gallery is for you. Admission is free.

↓ HUGH LANE GALLERY

↓ IMMA

Museum of Literature Ireland (MoLI)

86 St. Stephen's Green, City Centre, Dublin 2, moli.ie

In a city that boasts four Nobel writers and an impressive list of internationally acclaimed novelists, poets, and playwrights, a museum dedicated to literature is right where it belongs. The museum, featuring interactive exhibitions, is located in a historic University College Dublin building along St. Stephen's Green. James Joyce once studied here, and you can even see the first copy of his famous *Ulysses* on display. Don't miss the courtyard and the lovely Readers' Garden, with the ash tree where Joyce had his graduation photo taken in 1902.

Chester Beatty

Dublin Castle, City Centre, Dublin 2, chesterbeatty.ie

Named after Sir Alfred Chester Beatty (1875–1968), an American philanthropist, mining magnate, and passionate collector of books, manuscripts, prints, and objects from Europe, Africa, Asia, and the Middle East, this museum showcases his incredible donations, including some very rare books and treasures. You'll find it right in the heart of the city, on the historic grounds of Dublin Castle. Free admission.

The Little Museum of Dublin

15 St. Stephen's Green, City Centre, Dublin 2, littlemuseum.ie

If you're in need of a good laugh, make your way to this delightfully quirky Dublin history museum. It's unlike anything you've seen before. In just 29 minutes (!), the guide will fill you in on everything from potatoes to U2, religion, and all the weird and wonderful bits of Irish history you didn't know you needed. It's history, but with a punchline. Great storytelling, sharp humour, and far from boring. It's best to book your tickets online.

Photo Museum Ireland

Meeting House Square, Temple Bar, Dublin 2, photomuseumireland.ie

Located in the heart of the bustling Temple Bar district, this small modern museum dedicated to Irish contemporary photography offers a welcome retreat from the crowds. Offering five to six engaging exhibitions annually, along with conversations with photographers, fun workshops, and a great bookshop, it's a must-visit for photography enthusiasts. The venue is also home to the Photo Museum Ireland Collection, an important archive dedicated to contemporary Irish photographers. Free admission.

National Gallery of Ireland

Merrion Square West, South-East Inner City, Dublin 2, nationalgallery.ie

Spread across three floors, this spacious museum is home to an outstanding collection of Irish and European art, from around 1300 to today. You'll find big names like Caravaggio, Rembrandt, Monet, and Picasso alongside loads of other fascinating artists. There are also some free tours available, and admission is free for the permanent collection and some temporary exhibitions.

↓ PHOTO MUSEUM IRELAND

National Museum of Ireland, Collins Barracks

Collins Barracks, Benburb Street, Stoneybatter, Dublin 7, museum.ie

Set in a stern-looking former military building, this museum brings together two very different collections: Decorative Arts & Design and Military History. One of the highlights is the permanent exhibition on Eileen Gray, the avant-garde 20th-century Irish designer and artist. Curious about Ireland's military past? Don't miss the *Soldiers and Chiefs* exhibition. Free admission.

Kilmainham Gaol Museum

Inchicore Road, Kilmainham, Dublin 8, kilmainhamgaolmuseum.ie

Kilmainham Gaol, Dublin's historic jail, opened in 1796 and closed in 1924. It once held everyone from common criminals to key figures in the fight for Irish independence. In the early days, people were even hanged here, and during the Great Famine, many were jailed simply for begging or stealing food. Men and women were locked up together until 1881, when it became a men-only prison. You can only visit on a guided tour, and tickets need to be booked in advance, so plan ahead!

Irish Museum of Modern Art (IMMA)

Royal Hospital, Military Road, Kilmainham, Dublin 8, imma.ie

IMMA holds an impressive collection of modern and contemporary works. It also hosts engaging talks, workshops, tours, and more. The museum is set in the Royal Hospital Kilmainham, a monumental 17th-century building inspired by Les Invalides in Paris, with a courtyard. Your visit isn't complete without a stroll through the gardens and surrounding meadows. Free admission.

NATIONAL GALLERY OF IRELAND

STREET ART

Irish street art historically focused on slogans and political messages, but the last few years have seen the rise of beautiful works that serve a more decorative purpose. In Dublin, you really don't need to make an effort to find amazing street art. Temple Bar, in the heart of the city, is full of colourful works. But there is so much more to discover. Hunting for street art tends to bring you to the more creative outskirts of a city: it is the perfect way to get off the beaten track. Most artworks are not enclosed, nor protected, so check whether a specific work still exists before going to see it. You can use a phone app like *Street Art Cities* or join a street art tour to make sure you will see the best pieces.

Traffic light boxes

These grey boxes found all over Dublin have become part of a community art project. Follow the hashtag *#DublinCanvas* and you'll find over 750 boxes that have been transformed into artworks by a diverse group of Irish and international artists.

Pass freely

O'Connell Street, North City, Dublin 1

A collaboration between Hugh Lane Gallery and artist Asbestos, this large mural is a tribute to people who lost their lives due to COVID. The mural is composed of over 5,000 individually painted matches, representing the lives of Irish COVID victims. A large text reads 'pass freely from one level of existence to another', which is a quote from *The Secret Block for a Secret Person in Ireland* by Joseph Beuys.

Writer's Block

20 Richmond Cottages, Summerhill, North City, Dublin 1

On the side of Richmond Cottages in Summerhill, the mural *Writer's Block* honours writer Brendan Brehan, an icon of the city who is closely associated with the Northside. Artist Shane Sutton portrayed him deep in thought with a typewriter and an emptied pint.

Young James Joyce

20 Richmond Cottages, Summerhill, North City, Dublin 1

Just a few houses over, another Shane Sutton mural depicts a young James Joyce, who lived at 17 North Richmond Street for some time and set his short story *Araby* in this very area.

Blooms Hotel

3-6 Anglesea Street, Temple Bar, Dublin 2

The entire exterior of the Blooms Hotel is covered in a vibrant mural celebrating James Joyce's famous novel *Ulysses*. The detailed artwork, made by artist James Earley, features characters from the book, like Molly and Leopold Bloom, Stephen Dedalus and Buck Mulligan, surrounded by a brightly coloured abstract-psychedelic design.

Shelbourne Racecourse

South Lotts Road, Ringsend, Dublin 4

Danni Simpson, an Australian artist living in Belfast, has created numerous large works around the world. She also painted several stunning pieces in Dublin. Some of her latest works, a collaboration with Irish street artist Karl Fenz, can be found at the Shelbourne Park Greyhound Stadium. They combined their two styles into impressive large-scale greyhounds, which are there to brighten up your day.

U Are Alive

4 Grantham Street, Saint Kevin's, Dublin 8

Made by internationally acclaimed Dublin street artist Maser, this mural on the corner of Grantham and Camden Street is one of his most iconic works. It is a reminder to be present, appreciate your surroundings, and find joy in everyday life.

James Joyce Quote

27 Harman Street, Saint Catherine's, Dublin 8

'They lived and laughed and loved and left,' a quote from James Joyce's *Finnegans Wake*, has been painted onto a gable wall on Harmon Street by Garreth Joyce and Vanessa Power of Signs of Power. Commissioned by the board of St. Teresa's Gardens, the quote is meant to capture the shift in demographics in the area.

↓ PASS FREELY ASBESTOS X HUGH LANE GALLERY

CINEMA & THEATRES

The Abbey Theatre

26-27 *Abbey Street Lower, North City, Dublin 1, abbeytheatre.ie*

The National Theatre of Ireland, the Abbey, was founded in 1904 and has hosted many of Ireland's renowned playwrights and actors. Their mission is to inspire Irish society through the country's large canon of Irish playwriting.

The Gaiety Theatre

King Street South, City Centre, Dublin 2

Opened in 1871 and still in operation, the Gaiety Theatre remains Dublin's main venue for musicals, opera, concerts, and more, featuring a Victorian interior.

Bord Gáis Energy Theatre

Grand Canal Square, Docklands, Dublin 2, bordgaisenergytheatre.ie

Designed by architect Daniel Libeskind, this theatre is a landmark in Dublin's Docklands, showcasing everything from Broadway and West End shows to local and independent productions.

Irish Film Institute

6 Eustace Street, Temple Bar, Dublin 2, ifi.ie

Ireland's moving image heritage is preserved and made accessible to all at the Irish Film Institute. They show Irish and international films, with a mix of new and classic titles.

Stella Cinema

207-209 Rathmines Road Lower, Rathmines, Dublin 6 & 117-119 Ranelagh, Dublin 6, stellacinemas.ie

Originally opened in 1923, this one-screen cinema offers a luxurious experience in a historic setting, with food and drinks served at your seat. They show both new releases and Hollywood classics.

Light House Cinema

Market Street South, Smithfield, Dublin 7. lighthousecinema.ie

A unique and artistic cinema with a diverse programme, from blockbusters to indie films and international releases. They also host events such as book clubs, quiz nights, and special screenings.

↓ THE GAIETY THEATRE

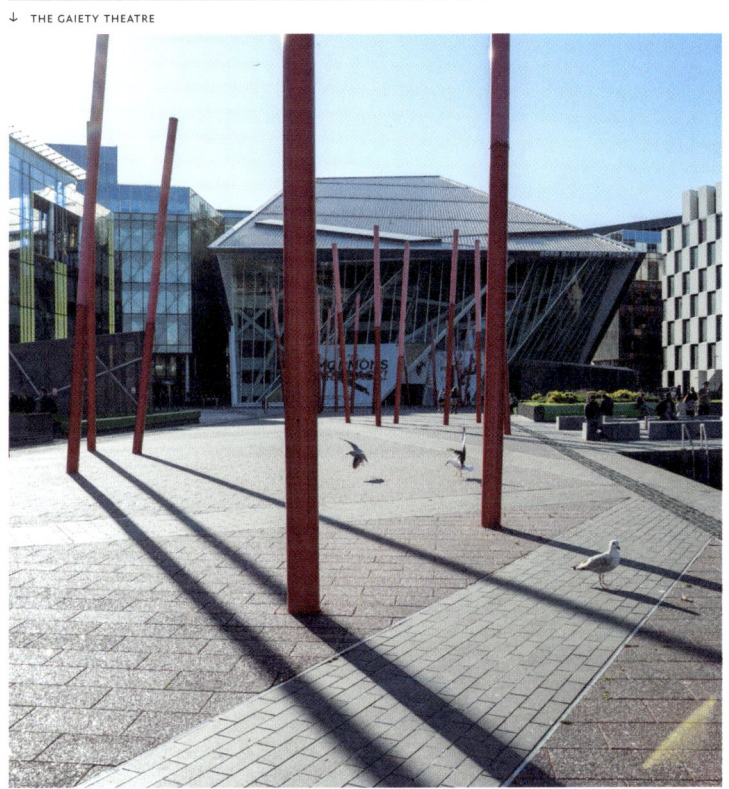

CINEMA & THEATRES

FESTIVALS

Tradfest

This yearly festival celebrates Irish music and culture. Over five days in January, the city fills with live music, from intimate pub gigs to major performances in historic venues like St. Patrick's Cathedral.

tradfest.com

Dublin International Film Festival (DIFF)

DIFF is a must for film fans. For eleven days in February, you can immerse yourself in movies and short films from around the world, enjoy red carpet premieres, and take in fascinating conversations with special guests.

diff.ie

St. Patrick's Festival

St. Patrick's Festival in March spans three days and is one of Dublin's biggest events. Expect lively parades with marching bands, street performances, live music, packed pubs, and a buzzing atmosphere.

stpatricksfestival.ie

International Literature Festival Dublin (ILFD)

In a country that cherishes its writers and holds reading close to the heart, the International Literature Festival Dublin is perfectly at home. Each May, Merrion Square comes alive for ten days with readings, debates, live podcasts, and more.

ilfdublin.com

Dublin Dance Festival

For two weeks in May, this festival brings the best of Irish and international contemporary dance to stages all over the city, showcasing bold, creative performances and choreography.

dublindancefestival.ie

Forbidden Fruit Festival

Traditionally held over the June bank holiday, this music festival takes place at the Museum of Modern Art and the Royal Hospital Kilmainham grounds, just outside the city centre. The lineup is packed with mostly electronic music and plenty of danceable beats.

forbiddenfruit.ie

Dublin Pride

One of the biggest LGBTQ+ festivals in the country takes over Dublin every year at the end of June, with a vibrant parade, parties all around town, and more fun events.

dublinpride.ie

Longitude

This three-day July festival is all about music and non-stop partying at the foot of the Dublin Mountains in Marlay Park. Expect big-name Irish and international artists across electronic, hip hop, R&B, and much more.

longitude.ie

The Big Grill

Held in the lush and leafy Herbert Park, this annual festival in August focuses on great food and good vibes. Irish and international chefs, together with BBQ pros, serve up their best dishes while live music and DJs keep the energy going.

biggrillfestival.ie

Dublin Fringe Festival

This August festival lights up venues all across the city with boundary-pushing theatre, high-energy dance performances, striking art installations, and unforgettable party nights.

fringefest.com

DUBLIN TOURS

Dublin Literary Pub Crawl

A tour of four lesser-known Dublin pubs once frequented by literary greats like James Joyce, Oscar Wilde, and Samuel Beckett. Led by professional actors (no cheesy costumes!) who tell the pubs' stories while quoting famous works.

9 Duke Street, City Centre, Dublin 2, dublinpubcrawl.com

Windmill Lane Recording Studios

Step into the studios where legendary artists have recorded, from Irish icons like U2 and The Cranberries to global stars like The Rolling Stones, Lady Gaga, and Ed Sheeran.

20 Ringsend Road, Ringsend, Dublin 4, windmilllanerecording.com

Jameson Distillery

Founded by John Jameson in 1780, this now world-famous distillery offers more than just a tour. You can also join a cocktail workshop or tasting session or learn how to blend your own whiskey.

Bow Street, Smithfield, Dublin 7, jamesonwhiskey.com

Roe & Co Distillery

Founded by George Roe in the 19th century, this whiskey distillery was once the largest in Ireland. It's still active and offers tours of the Still House, including a cocktail, or whiskey blending and tasting workshop.

92 James's Street, The Liberties, Dublin 8, roeandcowhiskey.com

Guinness Storehouse

Discover how Ireland's most famous drink is made through an immersive experience, ending with a pint of Guinness at the Gravity Bar with its panoramic views.

St. James's Gate, The Liberties, Dublin 8, guinness-storehouse.com

Glasnevin Cemetery Tours

Glasnevin Cemetery is the final resting place of Irish icons like Daniel O'Connell, Michael Collins, and Éamon de Valera. Guided tours on Irish history are available, as well as self-guided and audio options.

Finglas Road, Glasnevin, Dublin 11, dctrust.ie

↓ ROE & CO DISTILLERY

↓ GUINNESS STOREHOUSE

↓ AVIVA STADIUM

THINGS TO DO

City Kayaking

Want to explore Dublin from a different point of view? With City Kayaking, you can paddle under the famous O'Connell and Ha'Penny bridges and take in the sights along the River Liffey. Suitable for all levels of experience.

Liffey Boardwalk, Bachelors Walk, North City, Dublin 1, citykayaking.com

Museum Building at Trinity College

Although it is located in the heart of the famous Trinity College, this building remains relatively unknown. Built between 1853 and 1857, it features detailed carvings and a stunning main hall. You can visit by joining a Trinity Trails tour.

1 Park Lane East, South-East Inner City, Dublin 2, visittrinity.ie/trinity-trails

Croke Park

Ireland's largest stadium, Croke Park, is home to the Gaelic Athletic Association (GAA), the country's largest sports organisation, which represents the national sports of hurling and Gaelic football. You can watch a game, visit the GAA museum, or take a stadium tour.

Jones' Road, Drumcondra, Dublin 3, crokepark.ie

Rugby match at Aviva Stadium

Rugby is one of the most popular sports in Ireland, with a successful national team. You can watch a match at the Aviva Stadium, the home of Irish rugby and football, surrounded by suburban streets.

Lansdowne Road, Ballsbridge, Dublin 4, avivastadium.ie

Vicar Street

Vicar Street is a popular events venue in Dublin known for its intimate atmosphere and top-quality performances. It hosts a wide range of shows, from concerts to stand-up comedy and theatre, with both Irish and international acts.

58-59 Thomas Street, The Liberties, Dublin 8, vicarstreet.com

Blackrock Market

This small market in the seaside village of Blackrock is one of Dublin's oldest markets, established in 1986. It has over thirty stalls, ranging from antiques and clothes to food stalls, cafés, and even a Michelin-starred restaurant. Open on weekends.

19A Main Street, Blackrock, County Dublin, theblackrockmarket.com

Big Style Stand Up Paddle

One of the best ways to explore Dublin's coastline is from the water, and what better way than by paddleboard? Head out by yourself if you have previous experience, or join a guided tour to learn the basics.

Coal Harbour, Dún Laoghaire, County Dublin, bigstyle.ie/paddle-boarding-dublin

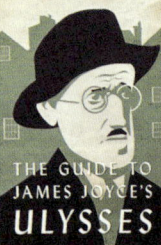

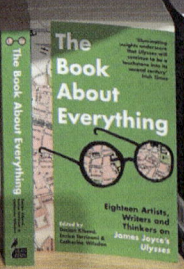

FAMOUS PEOPLE

Bob Geldof

Irish singer Bob Geldof is best known for his humanitarian work and activism. He co-founded Band Aid, the charity supergroup behind the iconic single *Do They Know It's Christmas?* and went on to organise Live Aid in the 1980s. These landmark musical events raised millions to fight famine in Africa. Born and raised in Dún Laoghaire, a coastal town in the south of Dublin, Geldof first rose to fame in the 1970s as the lead singer of the Dublin-based rock band The Boomtown Rats, best known for their global hit *I Don't Like Mondays*.

Bono

Who doesn't know the world-famous lead singer of U2? Dubliner Paul Hewson rose to global fame as Bono, not only for his musical performances, including his appearance at Band Aid, but also for his tireless activism. As a passionate advocate in the fight against HIV and AIDS in Africa, Bono has earned numerous awards and honours for both his musical and humanitarian efforts. He has even been nominated multiple times for the Nobel Peace Prize. In recognition of his contributions, he received an honorary knighthood from the British queen. Bono still resides in a village just south of Dublin, staying close to his Irish roots.

Cillian Murphy

This award-winning Irish actor has starred in numerous acclaimed films, including *28 Days Later*, *Oppenheimer*, *Breakfast on Pluto*, and *Small Things Like These*. Cillian Murphy is also widely known for his iconic portrayal of Tommy Shelby in the hit series *Peaky Blinders*. Although he wasn't born in Dublin, he now resides in the south of the city, in the scenic coastal village of Monkstown.

Eve Hewson

Known for her numerous roles in both film and television, including *The Perfect Couple*, *Robin Hood*, *Bad Sisters*, and *This Must Be the Place*, Eve Hewson has carved out a distinctive path in the film industry. Raised in Killiney, a suburb south of Dublin, she is the daughter of U2 frontman Bono. Despite her international success, she continues to call her childhood neighbourhood home.

Francis Bacon

Although Francis Bacon was born in Dublin in 1909 and his London studio was transferred to the Hugh Lane Gallery in Dublin after his death, he was British by nationality. The troubled painter developed a distinctive style later in life characterised by raw, dark, and provocative imagery featuring distorted figures and faces. He is widely regarded as one of the most important painters of the 20th century.

James Joyce

When you say Dublin, you say literature, and James Joyce. His masterpiece *Ulysses*, set in Dublin, is often regarded as one of the most important books of all time. Although Joyce was born in Dublin in 1882, he spent much of his life abroad. Nevertheless, Dublin remains central to most of his work.

Oscar Wilde

Another world-famous writer from Dublin is Oscar Wilde. Known for his eccentric flamboyant style, Wilde was not just an author but also a poet and playwright. He was born in Dublin in 1854 and grew up mostly at Merrion Square, right near where his statue stands today. He studied at Trinity College before heading off to Oxford. One of his most famous works is *The Picture of Dorian Gray*. Today, Wilde is an important figure in the LGBTQ+ community, as he was a queer man who paid a steep price for being himself in a time when society refused to accept this.

Paul Mescal

The Irish actor is best known for playing Connell Waldron in the miniseries *Normal People,* as well as starring in acclaimed films like *The Lost Daughter*, *Aftersun*, and *All of Us Strangers*. His connection to Dublin? He studied acting at The Lir Academy, part of Trinity College Dublin.

Sally Rooney

Although Rooney wasn't born and raised in Dublin, she studied at Trinity College. An internationally bestselling Irish author and screenwriter, she is one of the most renowned millennial writers. She is best known for her acclaimed works *Conversations with Friends*, *Normal People*, and *Intermezzo*. Her writing has earned her numerous prestigious awards.

Saoirse Ronan

This American-born Irish actress moved back to Ireland at the age of three and spent her teenage years in Howth, north of Dublin. At just 13, Ronan earned her first Oscar nomination for Best Supporting Actress for her role in *Atonement*. Since then, she has starred in numerous acclaimed films, including *The Lovely Bones*, *Brooklyn*, *Lady Bird* – which earned her a Golden Globe – and *Little Women*. She is also known for her roles in Wes Anderson's

The French Dispatch and *Grand Budapest Hotel*.

Sarah Bolger

Growing up in Rathfarnham, on the south side of Dublin, Sarah Bolger landed her first acting role at just six years old. Since then, her career has skyrocketed. She performed in both film and television, you might know her from her roles in *In America*, *Stormbreaker*, *The Spiderwick Chronicles*, *Once Upon a Time*, *The Tudors*, and the science fiction thriller *Descendent*. Recently, she starred as the cunning Emily Thomas in the hit series *Mayans M.C.* Though she spends much of her time in Hollywood, Bolger continues to live in the Dublin neighbourhood where she grew up.

Sinéad O'Connor

Sinéad O'Connor was a legendary Irish singer-songwriter and activist, born and raised in Dublin. With a voice unlike any other, she captured hearts. She grew up in the southside suburb of Glenageary and had a difficult childhood, which she opened up about in her memoir *Rememberings*. She rose to international fame with the powerful song *Nothing Compares 2 U*. In 1992, she made headlines when she tore up a photo of Pope John Paul II on Saturday Night Live to protest abuse within the Catholic Church. Sinéad sadly passed away at the young age of 56.

FILMS & SERIES IN AND ABOUT DUBLIN

My Left Foot (1989)

This Oscar-winning film, starring Daniel Day-Lewis, remains a must-see. It tells the true story of Christy Brown, who was born with cerebral palsy and could only control his left foot. Raised in a working-class Dublin neighbourhood, Christy defied the odds to become a writer and artist, using his left foot to create his work. Notable filming locations include the streets around Kilmainham Gaol and the area near St. Patrick's Cathedral, both of which serve as the neighbourhood Christy grew up in.

In the Name of the Father (1993)

This compelling film, starring Daniel Day-Lewis, Pete Postlethwaite, and Emma Thompson, is based on the true story of the Guildford Four: four Irish men who were falsely accused of the 1974 IRA bombings of the Guildford Pub in London and unjustly imprisoned for fifteen years. The prison scenes were filmed at Kilmainham Gaol in Dublin, which stood in for Park Royal Prison in London. Additional filming took place at Ardmore Studios in Bray.

Braveheart (1995)

Fourteen of the twenty filming locations for box-office hit *Braveheart*, starring Mel Gibson, were shot in Ireland. The film tells the story of a 13th-century Scottish warrior who leads the fight for Scottish independence. Among the stunning Irish locations featured are the Wicklow Mountains National Park, just south of Dublin. The Sally Gap and Glencree Valley provided some of the film's epic landscape shots and scenes of armies on the move, while Blessington Lakes was used for a few of the battlefield scenes.

Leap Year (2010)

This romantic comedy follows Amy Adams (Anna) as she travels to Dublin to propose to her boyfriend on Leap Day, in keeping with an old Irish tradition. Her journey takes an unexpected turn, sending her on a detour through the Irish countryside where she meets another prince charming, played by Matthew Goode. Filming locations in Dublin include St. Stephen's Green, Merrion Square, and the Temple Bar district.

Sing Street (2016)

What's not to love about this coming-of-age film set in Dublin that pays tribute to the 1980s? With a charming cast, sharp wit, and a soundtrack packed with iconic 80s hits, it's an endlessly entertaining journey from start to finish. Filmed on location in Dublin and its scenic coastal spots, such as Dún Laoghaire, Harbour East, and Dalkey Island, the movie beautifully captures the spirit of the time.

Dublin Murders (2019)

A psychological mystery and crime drama, this series follows two detectives as they investigate a pair of murders in Ireland's capital. Despite what the title might suggest, only parts of the show were filmed in Dublin. Most of the production took place in Belfast and across Northern Ireland. Dublin locations in the series include the village of Blackrock, the iconic red- and white Poolbeg Chimneys in Sandymount, and several streets in town.

Normal People (2020)

Who hasn't watched this highly acclaimed Irish drama series based on Sally Rooney's novel? It follows the complex relationship between Connell and Marianne, from their teenage years through university at Trinity College Dublin. The university scenes were filmed on location at Trinity College, while Marianne's house is on Wellington Road in Ballsbridge.

P.S. I Love You (2021)

This somewhat corny romance is based on a novel by the Irish writer Cecelia Ahern. The story follows a husband (Gerard Butler) who, after dying from an illness, sends his grieving widow (Hilary Swank) a series of letters written before his death to comfort her and encourage her to move forward. The film was shot both in New York and in Ireland. The Irish locations include the Wicklow Mountains, just south of Dublin, as well as several spots within the city, including Whelan's Pub in Portobello, where the couple first met.

Bad Sisters (2022-2024)

This Irish black comedy series is set against the backdrop of picturesque coastal villages along Dublin Bay, like Malahide and Skerries, as well as the iconic Forty Foot bathing spot in Sandycove. The story revolves around the five Garvey sisters, who may (or may not) have played a role in the mysterious death of John Paul, the cruel and controlling husband of one of the sisters. It's binge-worthy, blending suspense with sharp Irish wit.

Boyzone – Life, Death, and Boybands (2025)

Even if you weren't a big fan of the 90's boy band Boyzone (or haven't even heard of them), this three-episode documentary is still worth watching. It tells the story of five ordinary teenage boys from Dublin – Stephen Gately, Ronan Keating, Keith Duffy, Shane Lynch, and Mikey Graham – who were put together to form Boyzone. From the very beginning, their highly manipulative manager, Louis Walsh, was pulling the strings. His control over the group had far-reaching consequences, contributing to tensions within the band. The documentary shows the surviving bandmates reuniting to share the story of Boyzone, including the heartbreaking loss of Stephen Gately.

BOOKS IN & ABOUT DUBLIN

A Star Called Henry – Roddy Doyle

Henry Smart grows up in the slums of early 20th-century Dublin, a time marked by poverty and political turmoil. He takes part in the 1916 Easter Rising and tells his story, from his rough beginnings on the Dublin streets to his time as a fighter in the Irish Rebellion. It's a tale of wild adventures, heroism, and a touch of romance, all set against the backdrop of Ireland's struggle for independence.

Conversations with Friends – Sally Rooney

Sally Rooney's debut novel, published in 2017, follows Frances, a 21-year-old college student, and her best friend and ex-girlfriend, Bobbi, as they navigate life in Dublin. The pair become involved with an older married couple: Melissa, a photographer and writer, and Nick, an actor. When Frances begins a secret affair with Nick, it sets off a complex and emotionally charged journey through the shifting dynamics of love, friendship, and power.

Dubliners – James Joyce

James Joyce famously claimed that he always wrote about Dublin, so if you visit the city, you can't avoid him. If Joyce's epic *Ulysses*, describing a day in the life of Leopold Bloom wandering through Dublin, written in stream of consciousness, is too much for you, try the more accessible *Dubliners*. In fifteen short stories, Joyce depicts the lives of average residents in early 1900s Dublin and provides a commentary on the state of the country in a pivotal time in its history.

Our Song – Anna Carey

An ode to love lost and found, the joy of making music and the sweet memories of college life. It might sound like a story you've read before, but in the able hands of journalist and musician Anna Carey, the story of Laura and Tadhg wins over even the most unromantic cynic. Set against the backdrop of Trinity College in the early-2000s and north Dublin today, it tells the story of two former soul mates. One turned her back on a music career, the other has gone off to become a megastar. Then, sixteen years later, they have some unfinished business to resolve.

Scarlet Feather – Maeve Binchy

Culinary-school friends Cathy and Tom start a catering business. Not an easy feat when you're both in demanding relationships, have unsupportive, meddlesome families, and unexpected events turn your lives upside down. Full of characters, filled with plots and subplots, this book takes you to Dublin in the 1990s.

Time Pieces: A Dublin Memoir – John Banville

One of Ireland's greats has often been called a West Brit, because of the un-Irishness of the topics and the settings of his many books. Do get into his nominated and award-winning novels like *The Book of Evidence* and *The Sea*; there is a reason he has often been mentioned as a potential Nobel laureate. But when visiting, read his memoir *Time Pieces: A Dublin Memoir* about the time and the place that formed him, 1950s Dublin.

The Pull of the Stars – Emma Donoghue

Written in 2018–2019, but published in the early days of the COVID-19 pandemic, Donoghue takes you back a century, when the Spanish flu ravaged Dublin in the aftermath of World War I. Three women — a nurse, a doctor, and an untrained volunteer — find each other and a light in darkness, working in a place where some women fall victim to illness while others give birth.

The Red and the Green — Iris Murdoch

More than a book about an Anglo-Irish family with differing religious beliefs and nationalist preoccupations, Murdoch's *The Red and the Green* is a historical novel about the events and sentiments leading up to the Easter Rising of 1916.

The Speckled People — Hugo Hamilton

Not an easy read for several reasons, but definitely an insightful memoir when it comes to big themes like identity, nationality, family, and belonging. Hamilton paints the life of his young self as the child of a nationalist Irish father and a German mother who fought the Nazis. This dual identity didn't go down very easily in Dublin's streets back in the 1950s.

FUN FACTS

The Irish language

Irish English is full of unique words and phrases that locals use every day. *Craic* means fun or a good time; asking *What's the craic?* is like saying 'What's up?' The word *grand* is used to mean fine or alright. Finally, *sláinte* (pronounced slawn-cha) is a common toast, which means health.

The MGM Lion

The very first lion to roar for MGM, called Slats, was born in Dublin Zoo and starred in the studio's opening sequence from 1924 to 1928 (though he never actually roared on screen). Since 1957, another lion born in Dublin Zoo, named Leo, has taken over as the face of the iconic MGM logo.

St. Stephen's Green

Before 1663, St. Stephen's Green was far from the peaceful park it is today. Back then, it was rough common land used for grazing animals, public executions, and even the occasional witch burning. It was definitely not the ideal spot for a picnic it is today.

The longest pub lease

In 1759, Arthur Guinness signed a 9,000-year lease for the St. James's Gate Brewery – still the home of Guinness today – for just £45 a year. Talk about a bargain! It might just be one of the best business deals of all time.

Phoenix Park

Dublin's Phoenix Park is Europe's largest city park, covering

↓ TRINITY COLLEGE

↓ TRINITY COLLEGE

↓ THREE CASTLES BURNING

a massive 707 hectares. Originally a Royal Deer Park, it's still home to a herd of wild deer roaming freely. The park also contains Dublin Zoo, beautiful gardens, and Áras an Uachtaráin, the official residence of the President of Ireland.

The oldest pub

The Brazen Head is Dublin's oldest pub, with the current building dating back to 1754. Legend claims a pub has stood on this spot since 1198. While it's quite touristy today, it's still a great place to enjoy a pint and soak up over 800 years of history.

St. Valentine's remains

The remains of St. Valentine, the patron saint of love, were given to an Irish priest by Pope Gregory XVI in the 19th century. Today, they are kept in a secure vault beneath Whitefriar Street Church in Dublin. They are shielded from visitors, but there is a beautiful statue and shrine in the church that you can visit.

Three Castles Burning

The three castles on Dublin's coat of arms have been the city's symbol since the 13th century, but their true meaning remains a mystery. Some believe they represent the gates of the old Viking city; others think they're watchtowers guarding the walls. A popular theory is that it's Dublin Castle, repeated three times to reflect the mystical power of the number three.

Freedom of the City of Dublin

This honorary title has been awarded to a select few legends over the years, and it comes with ancient privileges. Most famously, it includes the right to graze sheep in St. Stephen's Green, which U2's Bono and The Edge have exercised.

Trinity College Dublin

Trinity is one of Europe's most prestigious universities, now sitting proudly in the heart of Dublin. But when it was founded, the city was much smaller, and the university was named Trinity College *near* Dublin. Times have definitely changed.

Number of pubs per resident

Despite its reputation as a pub-loving city, Dublin in reality has fewer pubs per resident than any other European capital.

O'Connell Bridge

This is the only traffic bridge in Europe that's wider than it is long. O'Connell Bridge measures about 45 metres wide and just over 44 metres long. Basically, it's more of a square than a bridge.

Snakes

If you go on a hike near Dublin, or anywhere in Ireland, there's one thing you'll never see: snakes! This absence is not due to St. Patrick driving them out as the legend suggests, but it's most likely a result of the last ice age. Rising sea levels cut Ireland off from Great Britain, preventing snakes from crossing over.

PHOTO SPOTS

Ha'Penny Bridge

In between North City, Dublin 1, and Temple Bar, Dublin 2

Built in 1816, the Ha'Penny Bridge was Ireland's first cast iron bridge and has since become a true symbol of Dublin. In the 19th century, pedestrians paid a halfpenny toll to cross — hence the name — but today, it's free for all. For the best shot, photograph the bridge from Bachelor's Walk or Wellington Quay, or stand on the bridge itself to capture the sweeping views of the River Liffey and the city skyline.

Dublin Doors

Fitzwilliam Square, Baggot Street and St. Stephen's Green

Dublin's Georgian streets and squares are lined with red-brick façades, uniform in shape and design, with few decorations or ornaments. To add a personal touch, residents began painting their front doors in bold colours, and they still do — making for one of the city's most iconic and photogenic sights. You'll find these colourful doors all over the city, but the best examples are around Merrion Square,

Synod Hall Bridge

*Winetavern Street,
The Liberties, Dublin 8*

This eye-catching covered bridge connects Christ Church Cathedral to the Synod Hall (currently Dublinia Viking Museum). Built as part of a reconstruction in the 1870s, it's a mix of Gothic and Victorian architecture styles, with intricate limestone details and arched windows with stained glass, making for a great shot.

The Temple Bar Pub

*47-48 Temple Bar,
Dublin 2*

One of Dublin's most photogenic (and well-known) pubs, The Temple Bar stands out with its bright red façade, traditional signage, and string lights that glow year-round. While it's always picture-worthy, the pub truly goes over the top for holidays, with Halloween spiders or Christmas trees covering the building. For the best photo, head over early in the day before the crowds arrive.

The Spire

*O'Connell Street Upper,
North City, Dublin 1*

At 120 metres tall, the Spire is the tallest stainless-steel monument in the world and Europe's tallest sculpture. This sleek, needle-like structure rises from O'Connell Street, narrowing from a 3-metre-wide base to just 15 centimetres at the tip. Photograph it from below to capture its height or frame it with the surrounding historic buildings for contrast. Or visit in the evening, when a beacon of light seems to shine from the top.

Trinity College Dublin

College Green, South-East Inner City, Dublin 2

With its beautiful historic architecture, getting the perfect picture is not hard at Trinity. Visit the iconic Long Room in the Old Library, with a vaulted wooden ceiling and rows of old books. Or capture the Campanile on the Front Square, a freestanding bell tower built in the 19th century. Arrive early or late in the day to avoid the crowds.

Sunrise over Dublin Bay

Watching the sunrise over Dublin Bay is a wonderful experience. The best places to capture it are Howth Summit, Killiney Hill, and the Poolbeg Lighthouse, each offering stunning panoramic views of the coastline. All three spots involve some travel and a bit of walking, so it's important to plan ahead. And of course, be prepared for a very early wake-up call!

Grand Canal Docks

Docklands, Dublin 2

A contrast to Dublin's historic centre, the Docklands are home to sleek modern architecture, with the occasional historic warehouse in between, making for great contrasting photos. The architectural landmark of the Bord Gáis Energy Theatre at Grand Canal Docks, along with the colourful neon street art in front of it, is especially photogenic.

Oscar Wilde Memorial

Merrion Square Park, South-East Inner City, Dublin 2

If you're a fan of writer Oscar Wilde, a visit to his colourful statue in Merrion Square Park, just steps from his childhood home, is a must. The quirky sculpture shows Wilde lounging on a rock, surrounded by stone pillars engraved with his famous quotes. Interestingly, his face is carved to look thoughtful on one side and amused on the other, a subtle nod to his divided sense of self.

Samuel Beckett Bridge

In between Docklands, Dulin 1, and Docklands, Dublin 2

Spanning the River Liffey, the Samuel Beckett Bridge is a modern icon of the city. Designed by renowned architect Santiago Calatrava, the bridge resembles the shape of an Irish harp, a national symbol. For the best photos, head to the north quayside near the Convention Centre for a full view, or visit after dark, when the lit-up bridge reflects in the water below.

BREAKFAST, BRUNCH & COFFEE

Mind the Step

Tucked behind the busy streets of North Dublin, this café annex dance studio creates an atmospheric home for both coffee and dance addicts.

24 Great Strand Street, North City, Dublin 1, mindthestep.ie

Brew Lab

This specialty coffee shop is known for its award-winning baristas and excellent coffee. Alongside the brews, you'll find delicious sandwiches and fresh pastries, making it a great stop for any time of day.

17 Redmond's Hill, City Centre, Dublin 2, insta @brewlabdublin

Kaph

In the middle of buzzing Drury Street, this café is great for a coffee and pastry when on a shopping spree. Take a seat upstairs and enjoy the homey atmosphere while overlooking the busy street.

31 Drury Street, Creative Quarter, Dublin 2, kaph.ie

3fe

With their house-roasted coffee beans, this is the place for real coffee lovers. Their brunch menu is great too. Branches of this modern yet fun café can be found all over Dublin, but it all started at the Lower Grand Canal location, a personal favourite.

32 Grand Canal Street Lower, Docklands, Dublin 2, 3fe.com

Brother Hubbard

There are multiple locations, but our favourite is their most recently opened Ranelagh site.

With a modern and trendy interior, the menu draws inspiration from modern Irish cuisine and places emphasis on local Irish produce.

27 Ranelagh, Ranelagh, Dublin 6, brotherhubbard.ie

Grove Road

A beloved coffee and brunch spot among the locals. This small café offers an array of creative dishes. The iconic Irish breakfast – with black pudding and fried eggs – is given a modern touch.

1 Lower Rathmines Road, Rathmines, Dublin 6, groverroadcafe.ie

Alma

This small café in the heart of Portobello is a great place for brunch. Focusing on local produce and Argentinian flavours, Alma makes sure to serve a contemporary yet unique meal.

12 South Circular Road, Portobello, Dublin 8, alma.ie

Bibi's Café

Tucked away in the heart of Portobello, this coffee and lunch café feels like a living room, complete with bookshelves, plants, and art. The cute terrace garden is a favourite spot to savour a coffee, a sweet treat, or one of their delicious dishes.

14B Emorville Avenue, Portobello, Dublin 8, bibis.ie

Groundstate Coffee Roasters

Far from your average location for a good coffee or breakfast, this eco-friendly café is serious about sustainability and quality. They roast their own beans and serve a variety of tasty vegetarian dishes. They also sell cool coffee packages to take home.

48-50 James's Street, The Liberties, Dublin 8, groundstate8.com

Two Pups Coffee

Known for its inventive dishes and a welcoming ambience, Two Pups Coffee is a great choice for breakfast or brunch. Don't miss out on their incredible sweet treats.

74 Francis Street, The Liberties, Dublin 8 & 30 Annesley Bridge Rd, Fairview, Dublin 3, twopupscoffee.com

Juice Yard

Get your healthy boost at this charming spot with a green façade in Drumcondra. From smoothies, shots, and protein shakes to açaí bowls and the crowd-favourite overnight oats – everything is made fresh and packed with vitamins.

92A Drumcondra Road Upper, Drumcondra, Dublin 9, juiceyard.ie

Hatch Coffee

This neighbourhood café has a modern and trendy vibe. They serve delicious coffee, treats and a great contemporary brunch. But what makes this place extra special? The ocean is just around the corner.

13 Main Street, Blackrock, County Dublin & 4 Glasthule Road, Sandycove, County Dublin, insta @hatchcoffee

BAKERIES

Russell Street bakery

Situated right next to Croke Park, at this bakery you'll find freshly baked bread, buttery, flaky pastries, and delicious coffee.

Russell Street, Mountjoy, Dublin 1, insta @russellst.bakery

Bread 41

Tucked under the railway behind Trinity College, this organic bakery is a staple for Trinity students and office workers. With its wide range of delicious pastries and loaves, we fully understand why.

41 Pearse Street, City Centre, Dublin 2, bread41.ie

Fable Bakery

You'll find this bakery inside a salad shop on Dawson Street. They offer a range of delicious pastries and buns that are prepared over three days.

3 Dawson Street, City Centre, Dublin 2, fable bakery.com

Una Bakery

This artisan bakery is a real asset to its neighbourhood. Their sourdough loaves and pastries are much-loved by Dubliners, and with good reason. You can also grab a good takeaway coffee.

116 Ranelagh, Ranelagh, Dublin 6, unabakery.ie

Elliot's

This micro bakery is one of the most aesthetically pleasing, with all the pastries beautifully laid out. Make sure to go in the morning to get their daily coffee-and-bun offer!

330 North Circular Road, Phibsborough, Dublin 7, elliots.ie

The Fumbally

The Fumbally truly has it all! It's not only a café but also a shop where you can buy freshly baked sourdough breads and cakes, local and organic produce, fermented foods, natural wines, and beautiful gifts. Whether you stop by for coffee, breakfast, or brunch, you're always in for a treat.

Fumbally Lane, The Liberties, Dublin 8, thefumbally.ie

STREET FOOD & FARMERS' MARKETS

The Place Proper Street Food

This small square of food trucks offers a wide variety of flavours from around the world, from Indian and Polish to falafel, burgers, and Thai. The food is budget-friendly, yet delicious and high-quality.

Grand Canal Street Lower, Docklands, Dublin 2, insta @placestreetfood

St. Anne's Park Market

Set in the heart of St. Anne's Park, this Saturday market is ideal for a weekend stroll with a bite to eat along the way. You'll find a great mix of handmade crafts, local produce, baked goods, and hot food – with plenty of vegan, vegetarian, and gluten-free options.

St. Anne's Park, Clontarf, Dublin 3,
insta @stannesparkmarket

Herbert Park Farmers' Market

Every Sunday, this market sets up in the charming Herbert Park with a variety of stalls offering local and organic produce, hot food, flowers, crafts, and more. Minutes from the Aviva Stadium, it's a perfect lunch stop before catching a match.

Herbert Park, Ballsbridge, Dublin 4,
insta @herbertparkfarmersmarket

Airfield Farmers' Market

Airfield Estate, Dublin's only urban working farm, hosts a farmers' market every Friday and Saturday, selling local produce, bread, jams, meats, and more. The estate also offers gardens, walking trails, a vintage car garage, and a restaurant. Perfect for a full day out.

Overend Avenue, Dundrum, Dublin 14,
airfield.ie

Dún Laoghaire CoCo Market

In the seaside village Dún Laoghaire, CoCo Market pops up in two spots every Sunday. The Lexicon area turns into a Food Village with hot meals, baked goods, and local produce, while the People's Park focuses on books, arts, and crafts. Both are well worth a visit.

The People's Park, Glenageary Road Lower,
Glenageary, County Dublin, dlrcoco.ie

Irish Village Markets

From Wednesdays to Fridays, this market appears at various locations across the city, offering a range of high-quality street food for the lunchtime crowd. From falafel and sushi to fish and chips, this market has something for everyone. Check their website for the latest locations.

irishvillagemarkets.ie

SWEET TOOTH

The Rolling Donut

A staple for Dubliners, this shop is known for its delicious, handcrafted sourdough and vegan doughnuts with creative flavours – think Kinder Bueno, salted caramel, and apple crumble. What started out as a small kiosk on O'Connell Street has now become a phenomenon that has since spread across Dublin.

6 O'Connell Street Upper, North City, Dublin 1, therollingdonut.ie

Cookieboy

For delicious homemade Korean cookies and speciality coffee, head over to Cookieboy. Their huge cookies in classic as well as innovative flavours are unlike anywhere else in Dublin.

20 Stephen Street Lower, City Centre, Dublin 2, cookieboy.ie

Murphy's Ice Cream

Murphy's aims to make the best ice cream in the world, avoiding artificial colourings and flavourings, making as much as possible from scratch, and using local ingredients like milk from the rare native Kerry cow. They even produce their own sea salt from Dingle seawater.

27 Wicklow Street, City Centre, Dublin 2, murphysicecream.ie

Scoop Dessert Parlour

Scoop's bright blue-and-red façades are hard to miss. With several locations throughout

cookieboy
Cookieboy

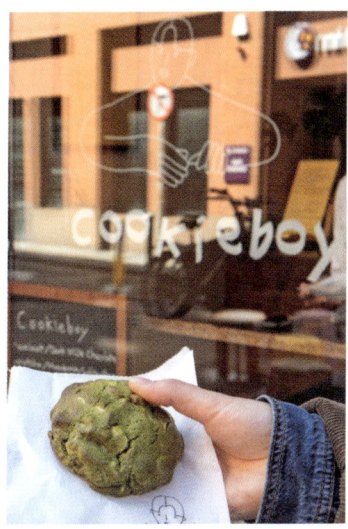

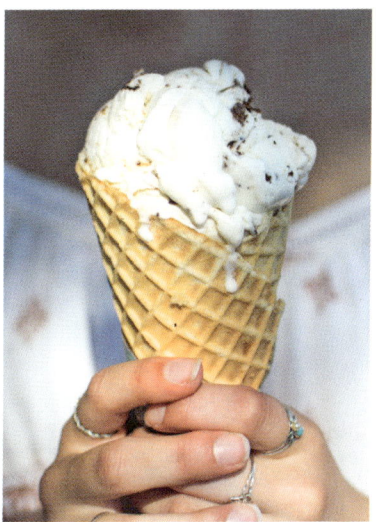

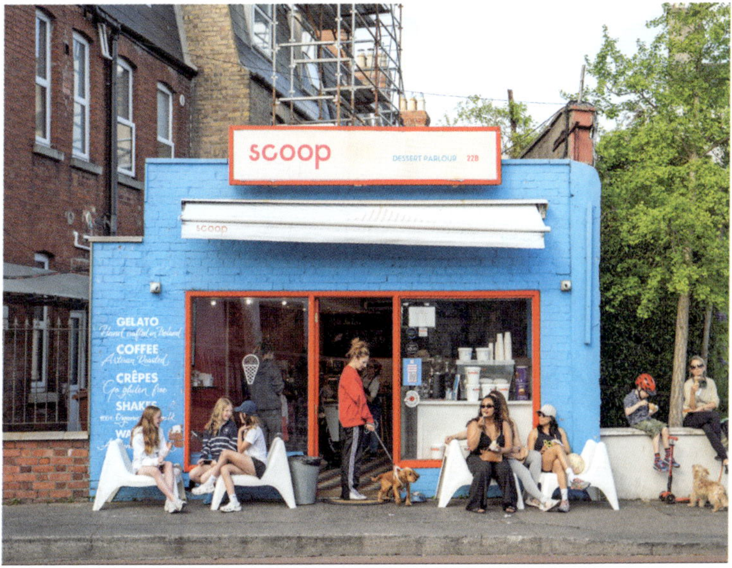
scoop
DESSERT PARLOUR 228
scoop
GELATO
COFFEE
Artisan Roasted
CRÊPES
Go gluten free

the city, they make sure there's always great ice cream nearby.

82 Aungier Street, City Centre, Dublin 2 & 22 Sandford Road, Ranelagh, Dublin 6, scoopgelato.ie

Spilt Milk

This small shop makes its ice cream in-house, using local ingredients. Their seasonal ice cream flavours make it a great spot all year. If you're in Dublin in winter, try their hot chocolate with marshmallow cream; it lives up to the hype.

30 Drury Street, Creative Quarter, Dublin 2, spiltmilkicecream.com

SLICES

A good slice of pizza is a favourite snack among Dubliners. You can find takeaway slices all over town. The Irish eat them with a dip. These are some great spots:

Doom Slice for thick, deep-dish Detroit-style pizza

14 Dame Lane, City Centre, Dublin 2, doomslice.pizza

DiFontaine's for a late-night New York-style slice

22 Parliament Street, Temple Bar, Dublin 2, difontainespizzeria.ie

Mani for Roman-style pizza

42 Drury Street, Creative Quarter, Dublin 2, manipizza.ie

Bambino for classic New York-style pizza

7 Stephen Street Lower, Creative Quarter, Dublin 2; 18 Merrion Street Upper, South-East Inner City, Dublin 2, bambino.ie

FISH & CHIPS

We all know the classic fish and chips from Ireland's neighbour, England. While first introduced to England by the Italians, the meal found its way to Ireland in the 1880s, where its popularity quickly caught on. It has been a staple in Irish cuisine ever since. The English go to 'the chippy' to have some 'fish 'n' chips', but the Irish go to the 'chipper' and ask for 'one and one'. Due to Ireland's Catholic heritage and the tradition of avoiding meat on Fridays, this is still a popular day to visit the local chipper.

Leo Burdock

As one of Dublin's most famous fish and chips shops, Leo Burdock has been a staple for Dubliners since 1913. There's often a queue, but the freshly caught, perfectly fried fish is worth the wait. At some of their locations you can eat in.

4 Crown Alley, Temple Bar, Dublin 2, leoburdock.com

Fish Shop

Want to enjoy your fish and chips with a glass of wine? This small but sophisticated wine bar, where you'll enjoy your food at a marble bar, is the place to go. It has a large assortment of natural wines, a changing daily menu, and, of course, delicious crispy, locally caught, beer-battered fish.

76 Benburb Street, Smithfield, Dublin 7, fish-shop.ie

Beshoff Bros

A staple among Dubliners, Beshoff Bros has been around for over 85 years. They aim to be as sustainable as possible. They fry their fish at multiple takeaway shops. On weekends, expect long queues.

12 Harbour Road, Howth, Dublin 13, beshoffbros.com

PUB GRUB

The Irish are all about comfort food: simple and straight to the point with dishes like shepherd's pie, beef and Guinness stew, bangers and mash, and fish and chips. These are the places to go for the best pub grub.

O'Neill's

As one of our favourite Dublin pubs, O'Neill's has it all: situated in an old, beautifully decorated building, this pub serves quality pints with live

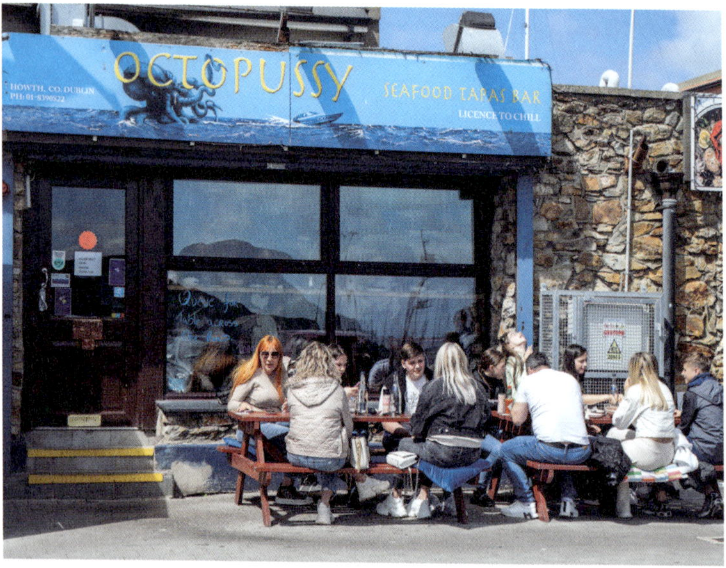
OCTOPUSSY
HOWTH, CO. DUBLIN
SEAFOOD TAPAS BAR
LICENCE TO CHILL

Loose Canon
CHEESE & WINE

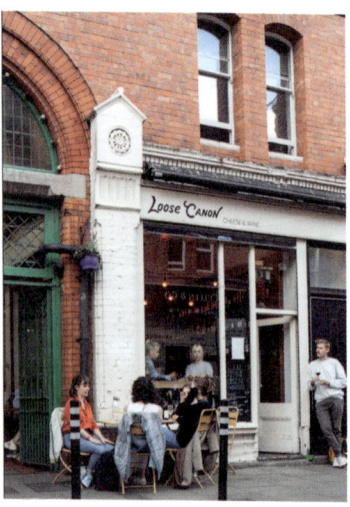

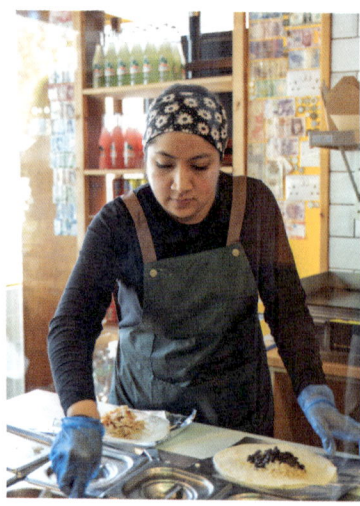

music seven days a week. But what sets this pub apart is their delicious food. Their shepherd's pie and beef and Guinness stew are superb.

2 Suffolk Street, City Centre, Dublin 2, oneillspubdublin.com

Darkey Kelly's

For the ultimate Irish night, this is the place to go. Sit down with a pint of Guinness and one of their delicious classic Irish dishes and listen to live traditional Irish music.

Fishamble Street, Temple Bar, Dublin 2, darkeykellys.ie

Lincoln's Inn

For a more refined, restaurant-like experience, go to Lincoln's Inn. Apart from quality pints, they serve classic dishes – and more. The famous author James Joyce used to come here often; it's also where he met his wife.

19 Lincoln Place, South-East Inner City, Dublin 2, lincolnsinn.ie

WINE BARS

Loose Canon

This charming little spot in St. George's Arcade is a wine and cheese shop and bar in one. At Loose Canon you can enjoy lovely natural wines, Irish cheese and, best of all, their renowned cheese toasties.

29 Drury Street, Creative Quarter, Dublin 2, loosecanon.ie

Two Faced

A name to take literally: this so-called 'café by day and wine bar by night' claims it never closes (though of course, it eventually does). Good coffee, a wide selection of wines, and a small but successful food menu, this spot never disappoints.

2 Montague Street, Saint Kevin's, Dublin 2, insta @twofaceddublin

LUNCH & DINNER

Bar Pez

Walking into Bar Pez feels like stepping into a tapas bar in Spain. The food, the lively atmosphere, and the friendly staff all create an authentic experience. The vibe may be Spanish; the ingredients and seafood are sourced locally.

Kevin Street Lower, Portobello, Dublin 8, barpez.ie

Xi'an Street Food

Xi'an's is *the* place to get a *spice bag*. Not commonly known among foreigners, this is the perfect fusion of Chinese and Irish culture. After a night out, few things hit the spot like a big bag of fried chicken and chips tossed in Chinese spices. No Irish student experience is complete without a spice bag from Xi'an's.

16 North Earl Street, North City, Dublin 1 & 8 Anne Street South, City Centre, Dublin 2, xianstreetfooddublin.ie

BIGFAN

This Chinese restaurant serves authentic Chinese cuisine with a contemporary twist. Their extensive menu is great for shared dining, with handmade dumplings, fresh bao, small bites, and larger dishes.

16 Aungier Street, City Centre, Dublin 2, bigfan.ie

Chimac

While travelling in Seoul, the owners of Chimac fell head over heels for Korean fried chicken, and they just had to open up a restaurant to sell this soul food from Seoul. Their chicken burgers, paired with one of their award-winning sauces, taste as good as they look.

76 Aungier Street, City Centre, Dublin 2, chimac.ie

Tang

Head to Tang right outside St. Stephen's Green for a nutritious, healthy, and delicious lunch. This corner café has excellent outdoor seating. You'll also find them at two other locations.

23C Dawson Street, City Centre, Dublin 2, tang.ie

Bunsen

A simple menu goes a long way. This is certainly true for Bunsen's classic, no-fuss, juicy burgers. Craving some? No problem. With several locations across the city centre, you'll never be far from a Bunsen.

3 Anne Street South, City Centre, Dublin 2 & 97 Ranelagh, Ranelagh, Dublin 6, bunsen.ie

El Silencio Fff

A speakeasy hidden behind the salsa shelves of a takeaway burrito shop. Ring the doorbell and find yourself in a vibrant Mexican *tequileria* with a great menu and some of the best margaritas you'll find in Dublin.

4 Clarendon Market, Creative Quarter, Dublin 2, insta @el_silencio_fff

Masa

Craving Mexican and looking for a more casual spot? This *taqueria* offers tasty, traditional, and affordable tacos and quesadillas in a hip and contemporary atmosphere.

2-3 Drury Street, Creative Quarter, Dublin 2 & 19 Camden Street Lower, Saint Kevin's, Dublin 2, masadublin.com

Mama's Revenge

A great spot to grab some tasty Tex-Mex burritos, quesadillas, and a cool beer, perfect for a picnic at the nearby Merrion Square or the Green at Trinity College. Students in Ireland can enjoy discounts on burritos!

12 Leinster Street, South-East Inner City, Dublin 2, mamasrevenge.com

Vice Pizza & Wing Shop

Vice has an unexpected yet exciting menu, serving delicious sourdough pizzas and crunchy chicken wings. Book a table in the basement, where mirrored walls create a fun, intimate atmosphere.

5 Merrion Street Lower, South-East Inner City, Dublin 2, insta @vicedublin

Nomo ramen

Right off busy Camden Street, this casual spot offers some of the best ramen in Dublin. These hearty bowls have been carefully tested and developed. Don't forget to try their bao buns. Oh, and do pick up a hoodie!

4 Charlottes Way, Saint Kevin's, Dublin 2, nomoramen.ie

Hang Dai

Start your night with a delicious Chinese meal and end with a party; it's all possible at Hang Dai. Enjoy their famous apple wood-fired Skeaghanore duck in metro carriage seating, then dance the night away to one of their DJs. A great spot for group dining with good value for money.

20 Camden Street Lower, Saint Kevin's, Dublin 2, hangdaichinese.com

Space Jaru

A casual restaurant with an open kitchen and a small shopfront, Space Jaru puts Korean food on the Dublin map. They serve both authentic Korean dishes and classics with a twist. Expect flavour-packed dishes and generous portions.

67-68 Meath Street, The Liberties, Dublin 8, jaru.ie

Shouk

If you're in the Drumcondra area – perhaps after a match at Croke Park – be sure to visit Shouk, a vibrant, laid-back spot serving colourful and delicious Middle Eastern cuisine. You'll find lots of vegetarian options too. They also have some great outdoor seating.

40 Drumcondra Road Lower, Drumcondra, Dublin 9, shouk.ie

Octopussy's Seafood Tapas

If you're looking for fresh seafood with a stunning ocean view, Octopussy's delivers exactly that. Their seafood tapas are made with fresh fish and local produce. A great place for lunch after walking the trail along the coast of Howth.

West Pier, Howth, Dublin 13, octopussy.ie

Little Forest

This small, homey restaurant in Blackrock serves modern Italian-inspired food. Using lots of fresh ingredients, they make tasty antipasti, fresh pasta, and wood-fired pizzas with a perfect crust.

57 Main Street, Blackrock, County Dublin, littleforest.ie

Kyoto Asian Street Food

Over at the coastal district of Dún Laoghaire, this hidden gem serves comforting, fresh, and tasty Asian street food in a small, casual space. Great value for money!

12 Patrick Street, Dún Laoghaire, County Dublin, kyotostreetfood.ie

BRING THE PARENTS

Hera

Hera is Drumcondra's new darling; a cool gastro pub serving Mediterranean-inspired snacks and small-but-hearty mains. Sharing is encouraged. Expect beautifully presented dishes, bold flavours, and attentive service.

58 Dorset Street Lower, Drumcondra, Dublin 1, junobar.ie

Suertudo

This restaurant proves that Mexican food can be truly sophisticated. In a relaxed, colourful setting, you'll enjoy beautifully presented small plates full of genuine flavour. Be sure to treat yourself to one of their excellent cocktails.

47 Ranelagh, Ranelagh, Dublin 6, suertudo.ie

Spitalfields

If you're craving elevated pub food in an authentic setting, Spitalfields is the place to be. Traditional Irish dishes, like *cock-a-leekie pie*, oysters, and devilled eggs, are served alongside more creative, modern dishes.

25 The Coombe, The Liberties, Dublin 8, spitalfields.ie

September

Beautiful Italian-inspired dishes in a casual, stylish space with sweeping views of the sea. What better place to bring your parents? If you're celebrating, order the chef's menu and let yourself be surprised. All pasta is homemade, and the wine list focuses on natural selections.

3 Bath Place, Blackrock, County Dublin, septemberdublin.com

PUBS

The Stag's Head

Named after the large stag head mounted above the bar, this pub dates back to the 1770s and remains a popular meeting spot for Dubliners. It's one of the city's best-preserved Victorian pubs. They host live traditional music and comedy nights several times a week.

1 Dame Court, City Centre, Dublin 2, stagshead.ie

Kehoes

Described as 'a country pub in the heart of the city', Kehoes was established in 1803. And this traditional spot has kept its authentic Victorian interior intact since the late 19th century. With its stained-glass windows, classic Irish snugs, and wooden partitions, the pub has a homely atmosphere – and the pints are top-notch too.

9 Anne Street South, City Centre, Dublin 2, kehoesdublin.ie

The Palace Bar

One of Dublin's great literary pubs, The Palace Bar was once a regular spot for some of Ireland's great writers and still boasts its beautifully preserved Victorian interior. Located between Temple Bar and Trinity College, it attracts a mix of students, office workers, and tourists.

21 Fleet Street, Temple Bar, Dublin 2, thepalacebardublin.com

The Old Stand

This pub with old-world charm has stood in the same spot on Exchequer Street for 350 years. Nowadays, it's a popular location to watch rugby, football, and other sports. They also serve some tasty sandwiches.

37 Exchequer Street, Creative Quarter, Dublin 2, theoldstandpub.com

The Rag Trader

What was once a fabric house in Dublin's former rag trade district is now a charming pub with a traditional feel and a diverse whiskey selection. They host live music on Wednesdays and Thursdays and have regular whiskey tastings. Don't miss their 'Rag Trader Handshake', a great combo deal for a pint and a shot of Irish whiskey.

39 Drury Street, Creative Quarter, Dublin 2, theragtrader.ie

O'Regan's

It may not be one of the classic Irish pubs, but O'Regan's is still worth a visit. There's live music three nights a week, including the very popular Tuesday jazz nights. They serve great cocktails and pour a decent pint too.

26-27 South Great George's Street, Creative Quarter, Dublin 2, oregansdublin.com

O'Donoghue's

One of Dublin's oldest pubs, with live traditional Irish music every night of the week. Musicians from across the country gather to share their love of Irish folk music. There's also a charming outdoor seating area.

15 Merrion Row, South-East Inner City, Dublin 2, odonoghues.ie

The Hill

This lovely neighbourhood pub in Ranelagh has the feel of a traditional Irish pub with a modern twist. A favourite among locals, The Hill hosts weekly quiz nights on Tuesdays and live music on Sundays.

1 Old Mountpleasant, Ranelagh, Dublin 6, thehillpub.ie

The Hole in The Wall

This pub's name comes from a tradition that lasted nearly a hundred years: British soldiers who weren't allowed to leave Phoenix Park could still get a beer through a hole in the wall. As one of the only pubs surrounding the park, it's also known as Dublin's longest pub.

345-347 Blackhorse Avenue, Phoenix Park, Dublin 7, holeinthewallpub.com

Fagan's

Fagan's has been serving pints since the early 20th century, and this is reflected in its classic interior with wood-panelled walls, stained glass, and open fireplaces. Several famous people have found their way to this pub, including former U.S. President Bill Clinton.

146 Lower Drumcondra Road, Drumcondra, Dublin 9, faganspub.ie

The Bernard Shaw

This is far more than just a pub. The Bernard Shaw is a lively cultural hotspot featuring street food stalls, art spaces, drag brunches, and live events. Though named for its original Portobello location, birthplace of playwright George Bernard Shaw, the new Drumcondra venue proudly carries on the spirit and legacy of the original.

Cross Guns Bridge, Drumcondra, Dublin 9, thebernardshaw.com

John Kavanagh The Gravediggers

On a quiet square beside Glasnevin Cemetery stands one of Dublin's oldest family-run pubs, where you'll often find three generations of the Kavanagh family behind the bar. It's a true traditional pub with no music, no TVs — just good pints and great conversation.

1 Prospect Square, Glasnevin, Dublin 9, john-kavanagh-the-gravediggers.menu-world.com

BEER BARS

The Bar with No Name

Despite what its name might suggest, this bar is known as 'Dublin's worst kept secret'. It's lively all day long, great for casual drinks and a bite to eat, and really comes to life on weekend nights with DJs, music, and a busy bar. It can be hard to find but just look for the wooden snail above the door, head up the stairs, and you'll step into a space that feels more like a house party than a bar.

3 Fade Street, Creative Quarter, Dublin 2, noname.bar

BrewDog Dublin Outpost

A massive red shipping container all the way at the end of Grand Canal Docks, BrewDog has two bars, 32 craft beer taps, a varied food menu, and a rooftop terrace, making it a great spot for groups. Don't miss their guided beer tasting.

4 Three Locks Square, Docklands, Dublin 2, drink.brewdog.com

Kodiak

Kodiak is a beer lover's haven, with a huge selection of craft beers, from sours and stouts to Belgians and IPAs. Their wood-fired pizzas, ranging from classic to creative, pair perfectly with whatever you're drinking.

304 Rathmines Road Lower, Rathmines, Dublin 6, insta @kodiak_rathmines

Fidelity Bar

This bar is set in a sleek, retro-inspired space with a vinyl soundtrack and rotating DJs. You'll find a changing selection of beers from Whiplash Brewery, creative cocktails, and delicious Chinese dishes from Sister 7, BIGFAN's sister restaurant.

79 Queen Street, Smithfield, Dublin 7, fidelitybar.ie

Bonobo

A quirky interior and a great beer garden in the back. Bonobo offers a wide range of beers on tap, from craft options to classics like Guinness and Hop House 13, so there's something for every taste. And they make wood-fired pizzas in-house that come with creative yet tasty toppings.

119 Church Street Upper, Smithfield, Dublin 7, insta @bonobo_smithfield

CLUBS & PUB-CLUBS

Many Dublin pubs and clubs close at 2.30am but there are some that stay open into the late hours. Head over to Harcourt Street if you're not ready for the night to end.

The Grand Social

At the foot of the iconic Ha'Penny Bridge, The Grand Social has become a landmark in the Dublin music scene, both for after-work drinks and great music gigs. Their three event spaces host everything from intimate shows to full-blown club nights.

35 Liffey Street Lower, North City, Dublin 1, thegrandsocial.ie

Wigwam

A staple in the underground and alternative music scene, Wigwam is known for electronic music nights. They host events almost every night of the week, including Stock Market Mondays, Drag brunches, Tiki Bingo, and Tropical Trivia.

54 Middle Abbey Street, North City, Dublin 1, wigwamdublin.com

Izakaya Basement

Located in the basement of Japanese sushi restaurant Yamamori, this underground bar comes alive at night. With both local and Japanese drinks, featuring DJs every night, this spot makes for a unique night out.

13 South Great George's Street, City Centre, Dublin 2, yamamori.ie/night-life

4 Dame Lane

Tucked away on Dame Lane, this pub-club has live music, great DJs on the weekends playing Indie, Electro, and Pop, and the best cocktails.

4 Dame Lane, City Centre, Dublin 2, 4damelane.ie

Bad Bobs

This traditional-style pub turns into a lively club at night. There are four floors with great live music, including DJs playing with a live saxophonist, and outdoor seating.

35-37 Essex Street East, Temple Bar, Dublin 2, badbobs.ie

The Workman's Club

This spot is a haven for music and art lovers. From live music and indie club nights to book readings and comedy shows, it all takes place in a well-preserved Working men's Club building from 1888, with original features still present.

10 Wellington Quay, Temple Bar, Dublin 2, theworkmansclub.com

Copper Face Jacks

Located on Harcourt Street in the city centre, 'Copper's' is one of Dublin's best-known late-night bars. If you want to sing along to all the classics late into the night, this is the place to go.

29-30 Harcourt Street, Saint Kevin's, Dublin 2, copperfacejacks.ie

Dicey's Garden

Another Harcourt Street favourite, Dicey's has a late bar, DJs every night of the week, affordable drinks, and a mix of indoor and outdoor spaces – hence the name – including a roofless dancefloor where you can party under the night sky.

21-25 Harcourt Street, Saint Kevin's, Dublin 2, diceysgarden.eticks.io

Hogan's Bar

Hogan's is a lively bar with large windows and outdoor seating on the street, a great spot for summer days. From Thursday to Saturday, head downstairs to Hogan's International Beat Basement, where DJs play late into the night.

36 South Great George's Street, Creative Quarter, Dublin 2, hogansbar.com

QUEER

PantiBar

A part of Dublin's LGBTQ+ scene since 2007, this small and stylish gay bar is owned by none other than drag royalty Panti. It's a great spot for after-work drinks during the week, with lively shows and parties taking over at weekends.

7-8 Capel Street, North City, Dublin 1, insta @pantibardublin

The George

As Dublin's oldest and biggest LGBTQ+ club, the George has been at the forefront of the LGBTQ+ scene for over thirty years and remains a staple in the city's nightlife scene. Their huge dance floor, drinks deals, and nationally recognised drag acts make for a great night out.

89 South Great George's Street, City Centre, Dublin 2, thegeorge.ie

Mother Club

For disco lovers, Mother is the place to be on Saturday nights. Taking over the venue at Lost Lane, this LGBTQ+ club night transforms the space into an old-school disco haven. Expect a mix of electronic beats, retro synth sounds, and all things disco, delivered by some of Dublin's best DJs.

Lost Lane, Adams Court, Grafton Street, City Centre, Dublin 2, motherclub.ie

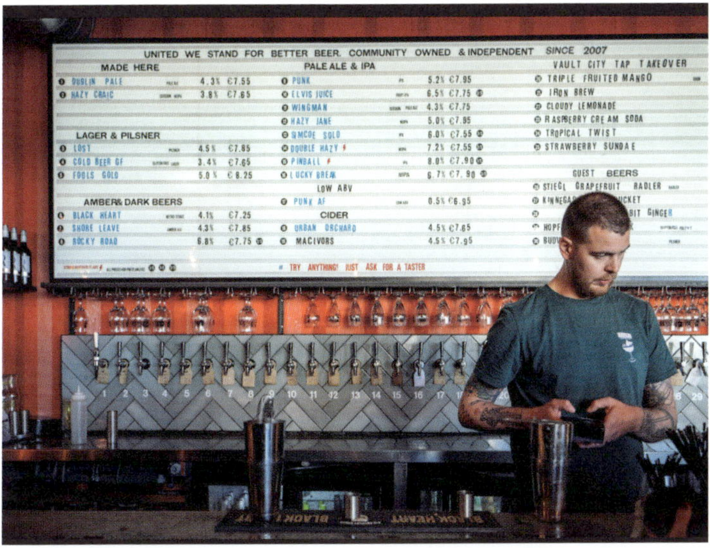

HOW TO DRESS LIKE A LOCAL

Dressing like a Dubliner is all about mastering the balance between casual, practical, and effortlessly stylish. You'll generally see locals in laid-back outfits, yet still looking put together, even when it's drizzling (which it often is). The weather in Dublin is famously unpredictable, so layers are your best friend. One moment the sun will be shining, while the next, it's pouring rain, so a solid waterproof jacket is a necessity.

When heading out to restaurants or pubs, don't overthink things. Most people keep it simple. That said, if you're planning a night out, you'll notice the girls often go all out, with heels, full glam, and bare legs, even mid-January. Still, no one will bat an eyelid if you show up in jeans and a nice top.

Traditional Irish fashion hasn't disappeared either. Wool knitwear and Irish scarves are still all around. But if you want to be like the hardcore Irish, pack swimwear – no matter the season. Many locals swim in the Irish Sea all year round.

With gorgeous coastal walks and mountain hikes all around Dublin, comfy shoes are a must. Dressed smart but ready for anything; that's the true Dublin look.

VINTAGE

Dublin Vintage Factory

1-2 Cope Street, Temple Bar, Dublin 2, dublinvintagefactory.com

Located in the heart of Temple Bar, Dublin Vintage Factory offers a unique shopping experience where clothes are sold by the kilo at €30. With two storeys of carefully selected vintage fashion from around the world, this shop is a haven for those seeking sustainable and affordable clothes.

Lucy's Lounge

11 Fownes Street Upper, Temple Bar, Dublin 2, insta @lucyslounge

Hiding behind a bubble-gum pink façade, this vintage wonderland is a kaleidoscope of eras and styles. The shop also houses Lucy's Lab, where clothes are upcycled and given a new life. For unique fashion finds, this shop is the place to go.

Nine Crows

22 Temple Lane South, Temple Bar, Dublin 2, insta @ninecrowstemplebar

Another Temple Bar favourite, the brightly coloured façade of Nine Crows is hard to miss. With one-of-a-kind handpicked pieces, this vibrant shop is a tribute to fashion from the 90s and 00s. Check their Instagram for restock dates to get first dibs.

Sacred Heart of Vintage

4 Temple Bar Square, Temple Bar, Dublin 2, insta @sacredheart_vintage

Tola Vintage

10 Fownes Street Upper, Temple Bar, Dublin 2, tolavintage.com

Continuing in her family's footsteps, founder Sophie McQuade opened her shop right above her father's vintage store. Sacred Heart of Vintage offers a selection of distinctive fashion pieces sourced from all over the world.

With multiple locations across the city, Tola has become a staple for vintage shopping in Dublin. They source unique 80s and 90s pieces from all over the world, selling items by weight at their shop in Aungier Street. If you're looking for more high-end pieces, their shop on College Green specialises in luxury brands.

The Big Smoke

Merchant's Arch,
Temple Bar, Dublin 2,
thebigsmokevintage.com

With a collection of pieces spanning from the 1960s to the 2000s, The Big Smoke's curated collection includes everything from retro jerseys and leather jackets to unique accessories. But their dedicated sportswear section sets them apart.

35 Vintage

13 Fade Street, Creative
Quarter, Dublin 2,
35vintage.ie

This vibrant shop is a go-to for vintage lovers. At 35 Vintage, you'll find a curated selection of pieces ranging from the 80s to Y2K. Whether you're hunting for a statement piece or simply browsing, there's something to suit your style.

Siopaella

29-30 Wicklow Street,
Creative Quarter, Dublin 2,
siopaella.com

Specialising in pre-loved designer handbags and accessories, Siopaella is a must-visit for fans of high-end fashion. This award-winning resale and consignment store in Dublin South also has a popular website and app.

Loot

23 Drury Street, Creative
Quarter, Dublin 2,
lootdublin.com

As a sister shop of Nine Crows, concept store Loot offers a curated collection of high-end vintage and contemporary fashion. They also sell magazines and host community events, making it a must-visit for fashion enthusiasts.

Lou's Lot

George's Street Arcade,
South Great George's Street,
Creative Quarter, Dublin 2,
insta @louslotshop

Looking for quality high-end vintage? Lou's Lot, tucked inside the historic George's Street Arcade, specialises in authenticated designer bags, accessories, and clothes. They only have a small selection of pieces at a time, so be sure to check their website for drop dates.

Betty Bojangles

77 Thomas Street, The Liberties, Dublin 8, insta @bettybojanglesdublin

Behind a Tiffany-blue shopfront lies a haven of vintage treasures. Inside, you'll find a mix of vintage, designer, modern, and new clothing and jewellery. It's a perfect spot to visit if you need something for a special occasion.

FLEA MARKETS

Temple Bar Book Market

2 Cow's Lane, Temple Bar, Dublin 2

Every weekend, Temple Bar Square transforms into a charming outdoor book market, with dozens of stalls offering a wide selection of books. You'll find everything from great Irish classics and modern novels to second-hand treasures, rare biographies and art books.

Le Zeitgeist Flea Market

Kelly's Yard, Phibsboro, Dublin 7, insta @ lezeitgeistfleamarket

Also known as the Bohemia Flea Market, this vibrant indoor and outdoor market brings together a diverse mix of stalls from all over the country, offering a large collection of vintage clothes, jewellery, art, homeware, and much more. Grab a coffee and a snack while you're browsing and enjoy live DJ sets playing in the background.

We LOVE Markets

The Digital Hub, 10-13 Thomas Street, The Liberties, Dublin 8, welovemarkets.ie

Held monthly at The Digital Hub campus, this open-air market has over fifty stalls and seems to grow with each edition. You'll find everything from vintage fashion and furniture to handmade crafts, artisan food, and more.

St. Patrick's Park Market

St. Patrick's Park, Patrick Street, The Liberties, Dublin 8, insta @ st.patricksparkmarket

Originally launched as a 'books and browsables' market, this Sunday event quickly grew in popularity and now features a wide range of handmade crafts as well. You'll find everything from second-hand books to sea glass jewellery and hand-poured candles.

ANTIQUES

Francis Street

Francis Street, The Liberties, Dublin 8, insta @dublinsantiquequarter

For those who want to spend their day shopping for antiques, Francis Street is the place to go. Dubbed the Art & Antiques Quarter, the street's shops offer everything from Georgian furniture and Irish silver to vintage jewellery and contemporary art.

STREETWEAR

High Rollers

65 Aungier Street, City Centre, Dublin 2, highrollersdublin.com

This skater-owned and operated shop is a skater sanctuary, selling everything from decks, trucks, and wheels to apparel from top brands like Nike SB, Polar, Palace, and Butter Goods.

Tribe Clothing

Unit 109 Stephen's Green Shopping Centre, City Centre, Dublin 2, tribe-clothing.com

This shop has been a staple in the Dublin streetwear scene since 1992. As Ireland's longest-running Carhartt WIP stockist, they offer a selection of skate, surf, and streetwear brands, including Vans, OBEY, Thrasher, and Rip Curl.

Saint Street Sneakers

9 Crow Street, Temple Bar, Dublin 2, saintstreet.ie

One of Dublin's go-to spots for streetwear and sneakers, Saint Street operates as a consignment shop, offering a selection of rare and sought-after items from brands like Supreme and Palace. The vibrant atmosphere and their commitment to authenticity make this shop a must-visit for those looking for distinctive fashion pieces.

Emporium

21 Drury Street, Creative Quarter, Dublin 2, emporiumdublin.com

Founded in 2018, this Dublin-born brand has become a key player in the city's streetwear scene. For local, high-quality streetwear, this is the place to go.

Genius Clothing & Footwear

6a, Powerscourt Townhouse Centre, Clarendon Street, Creative Quarter, Dublin 2, genius.ie

Specialising in contemporary men's fashion, Genius offers denim jackets, knitwear, and footwear from renowned European and global brands. Their mission is to provide clothing that combines practicality, comfort, affordability, and sustainability.

FASHION & DEPARTMENT STORES

Arnott's

12 Henry Street, North City, Dublin 1, arnotts.ie

Founded in 1843, this North Dublin department store is Ireland's oldest and largest. Offering everything from fashion and beauty to homeware and more, Arnott's remains a staple in the country's retail scene.

Brown Thomas

88-95 Grafton Street, City Centre, Dublin 2, brownthomas.com

Pop in for a moment and marvel at all the luxury items. This Grafton Street department store was established in 1849 and began as a modest drapery and haberdashery. Over the years, it has evolved into a multiple-story luxury store, offering high-end fashion, beauty, and homeware.

Powerscourt Townhouse Centre

59 William Street, Creative Quarter, Dublin 2, powerscourtcentre.ie

This grand 1774 Georgian townhouse is a piece of magnificent architectural heritage, with a beautiful Rococo style hallway and Neoclassical style interiors. Over the years, the building has evolved into a bustling shopping centre with over forty different eateries and shops offering a wide selection of Irish-made goods.

Dunnes Stores

Unit 10/11 Stephens Green Shopping Centre, St. Stephen's Green, Dublin 2, dunnesstores.com

First opened in 1944, this truly Irish department and grocery store now has locations all over the country. From clothes and homeware to groceries, Dunnes Stores offers a wide range of products at affordable prices.

FASHION & DEPARTMENT STORES

BOOKSHOPS

The Winding Stair

40 Ormond Quay Lower,
North City, Dublin 1,
winding-stair.com

This charming bookshop by the River Liffey pairs a wide book selection with an upstairs restaurant. Browse for books below, then head up the stairs for local, seasonal dishes and river views – this is a real Dublin gem.

Chapters Bookstore

Ivy Exchange,
Parnell Street,
North City, Dublin 1,
chaptersbookstore.com

Spanning two floors, Chapters offers a large collection of new and second-hand books across every genre, from fiction and history to art and cookbooks. With regular literary events as well, it's one of Dublin's most beloved independent bookshops.

Books Upstairs

17 D'Olier Street, City
Centre, Dublin 2,
booksupstairs.ie

Established in 1978 in an old hairdresser's salon upstairs from a furrier shop – hence the name – this beloved bookshop now spans three floors on D'Olier Street, offering a wide selection of new and second-hand books, and a charming café upstairs.

Hodges Figgis

56-58 Dawson Street,
City Centre, Dublin 2,
hodgesfiggis.ie

Founded in 1768, Hodges Figgis is Ireland's oldest bookshop and remains a favourite among readers as well as writers. The shop has been named in works by famous Irish authors such as James Joyce, John Boyne, and Sally Rooney, securing its reputation as a cultural icon.

Ulysses Rare Books

10 Duke Street, City Centre, Dublin 2, rarebooks.ie

Founded in 1969, this antiquarian bookshop has stayed in the family. They specialise in 20th-century Irish literature, including rare and first editions by Ireland's most famous authors such as Samuel Beckett, Oscar Wilde, W.B. Yeats, and James Joyce.

The Gutter Bookshop

Cow's Lane, Temple Bar, Dublin 2, gutterbookshop.com

This independent bookshop has a great selection of books, stationery, and gifts and is known for its staff picks and community events. The shop's quirky name comes from author Oscar Wilde's quote: 'We are all in the gutter, but some of us are looking at the stars.'

The Library Project

4 Temple Bar, Temple Bar, Dublin 2, thelibraryproject.ie

A great destination for contemporary art and photography lovers. This cool bookshop and gallery space offers a nice collection of art, photography, magazines, architecture books from both local and international artists, and much more.

Stokes Books

19 Market Arcade, South Great George's Street, Creative Quarter, Dublin 2, georgesstreetarcade.ie

It might not seem like it at first glance, but this small shop in George's Street Arcade houses a collection of over 10,000 antique and second-hand books. With a large variety of subjects and prices ranging from €5 to €5,000, the shop offers something for every type of reader – and budget.

The Last Bookshop

61 Camden Street Lower, Saint Kevin's, Dublin 2, insta @ thelastbookshopdublin

Books are everywhere in this second-hand bookshop. Lose yourself in the towering book stacks and then slip out the back to the Cake Café for the perfect coffee break.

MoLi Shop

Museum of Literature, 86 St. Stephen's Green, Saint Kevin's, Dublin 2, shop.moli.ie

The Museum of Literature Ireland has a charming shop that opens onto the museum's Reader's Garden. Inside, you'll find a curated selection of Irish-interest books, literary-themed gifts, and other unique items.

First Editions

7 Pembroke Lane, Pembroke, Dublin 4, firsteditions.ie

Specialising in rare and antiquarian books, First Editions has a selection of Irish literature, history, and poetry. This charming shop is a must-visit for collectors.

Hampton Books

93A Morehampton Road, Donnybrook, Dublin 4

Hampton Books is a beloved independent bookshop tucked away in the suburb of Donnybrook. In this small shop, you'll find a thoughtfully chosen range of titles, from the latest bestsellers to literary classics.

The Company of Books

96 Ranelagh, Ranelagh, Dublin 6, thecompanyofbooks.ie

This award-winning independent bookshop in Ranelagh is a favourite among Dublin locals, stocking a wide range of fiction, non-fiction and children's books.

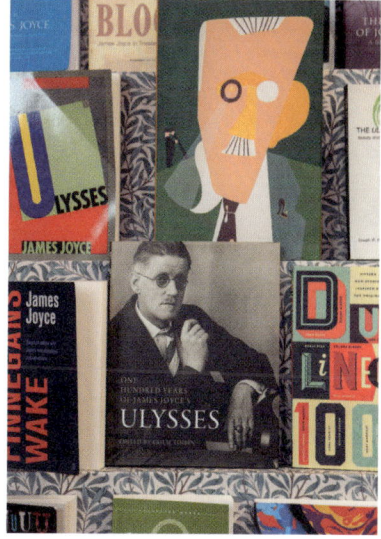

ART & CRAFT SUPPLIES

WM Trimmings

137 Capel Street,
North City, Dublin 1,
wmtrimmings.ie

If you enjoy knitting or sewing, this is your shop. WM Trimmings has been supplying Dublin with wool and fabrics since 1888. They offer a wide selection of yarn, fabrics, threads, buttons, and more – all at reasonable prices.

Yellow Brick Road

8 Bachelors Walk,
North City, Dublin 1,
yellowbrickroad.ie

This bead and crystal shop has a wide range of jewellery-making supplies, offering thousands of different beads in semi-precious stones, crystal, glass, wood, metal, and acrylic. They also host courses for anyone keen to learn.

CLOTH Dublin

Westbury Mall, Grafton
Street, City Centre,
Dublin 2, cloth.ie

Run by a mother-and-daughter duo, this fabric shop has a beautiful assortment of natural textiles – from Irish linen, wool tweed, and lace to Liberty of London cottons and silks.

Universal Art Supplies

12 Harcourt Street,
Saint Kevin's, Dublin 2,
universalartsupplies.com

Your creative spirit will come alive in this space. Established in 1887, Universal Art Supplies is a favourite among Dublin's artists. It has a wide range of fine art materials, from oils and watercolours to drawing tools and canvases.

Evans Art Supplies

5-6 Meetinghouse Lane,
Smithfield, Dublin 7,
evansartsupplies.ie

Evans Art Supplies has been around since 1910, back then selling packaging materials and paper. Over the years, the shop has expanded to meet the needs of artists, now selling a wide range of high-quality art materials.

MADE IN IRELAND

Jam Art Factory

14 Crown Alley, Temple Bar, Dublin 2 & 64/65 Patrick Street, The Liberties, Dublin 8, jamartfactory.com

For original Dublin souvenirs, go to Jam Art Factory. This family-run gallery and design shop sells art prints, ceramics, textiles, and jewellery created by talented local Irish artists.

Design Lane

2 Essex Street West, Temple Bar, Dublin 2, designlane.ie

The collection at this shop consists of 95 per cent Irish design, from prints and soaps to jewellery and clothing. Hats are crafted on-site by milliner John Shevlin, a James Joyce lookalike who's even made hats for the Irish president!

Article

Powerscourt Townhouse, South William Street, Creative Quarter, Dublin 2, article.ie

Elegantly set in Lord Powerscourt's former dressing room, Article offers a variety of home goods such as woollen throws, handmade candles, ceramics, prints, and even ostrich-feather dusters. They combine contemporary Irish design with finds from around the world.

Industry & Co

41 A/B Drury Street, Creative Quarter, Dublin 2, industryandco.com

Industry & Co is both a homeware shop and a café. Their trendy collection blends local Irish design with popular brands from Europe, the U.S.A., and Japan. Around the corner, on Exchequer Street, you'll find their lifestyle store and children's shop, Barn.

House of Wool

*13 St. Stephen's Green,
City Centre, Dublin 2,
thetemplebarshop.com*

Just outside St. Stephen's Green, this charming boutique offers one of the largest selections of 100% Irish-made hats, scarves, capes, and throws. Crafted from merino wool, mohair, and cashmere blends, their high-quality pieces are perfect winter staples.

VINYL & CDs

Tower Records

7 Dawson Street, City Centre, Dublin 2 & 40 Lower O'Connell Street, North City, Dublin 1, towerrecords.ie

Tower Records is Ireland's largest independent record shop. While its U.S. parent company has ceased trading, the Dublin store continues to thrive, offering a wide range of vinyl, CDs, DVDs, and Blu-rays while also regularly hosting live performances and signings.

All City Records

4 Crow Street, Temple Bar, Dublin 2, allcityrecords.com

This independent shop specialises in vinyl records and graffiti supplies, and has become a vibrant community of DJs, producers, and street artists. It has a strong selection of hip-hop, electronic, and experimental records, and even runs its own label.

The R.A.G.E.

8 Crow Street, Temple Bar, Dublin 2, therage.ie

The Record, Art, and Game Emporium is a paradise for retro enthusiasts. Alongside a solid selection of new and second-hand vinyl, they offer an impressive array of vintage consoles, games, controllers, and accessories.

Spindizzy Records

32 Market Arcade, South Great Georges Street, Creative Quarter, Dublin 2, spindizzyrecords.com

Spindizzy has been a staple in Dublin's music scene since the 90s. The independent shop offers a wide selection of new and used vinyl and CDs across genres — from rock and indie to hip-hop, jazz, and Irish traditional — and regularly hosts in-store gigs and signings.

SHOPS WE LOVE

Avoca

11-13 Suffolk Street, City Centre, Dublin 2, avoca.com

Avoca started in 1723 as a small weaving mill in its eponymous village of Avoca – a tradition that continues to this day. But it has grown into so much more. Whether you're after stylish clothes, unique Irish-made products, the perfect gift, or simply a great place to have lunch, this vibrant, multi-level concept store has it all.

Fresh Cuts Clothing

13 Castle Market, Creative Quarter, Dublin 2, freshcutsclothing.com

An Irish sustainable fashion brand for men, women, and kids. They design and print their own line of organic cotton apparel in Dublin. With a focus on timeless design and ethical production, Fresh Cuts provides quality garments that are made to last.

Irish Design Shop

41 Drury Street, Creative Quarter, Dublin 2, irishdesignshop.com

A celebration of Irish craftsmanship, this shop offers handmade products made by talented Irish designer-makers, including jewellery, ceramics, textiles, and homeware.

Wall & Keogh

45 Richmond Street, Portobello, Dublin 2, wallandkeogh.com

Entering this cute café and tea shop, you're surrounded by glass jars filled with premium loose-leaf teas. With over 150 high-quality options, from black and green to oolong, herbal, and fruity blends, this is tea heaven, with great coffee and snacks too.

Hopeless Botanics

Dean Street, The Liberties, Dublin 8, hopelessbotanics.ie

This vibrant plant and gift shop is a true sanctuary for plant lovers. It offers a selection of houseplants, dried flowers, botanical gifts, books, and art prints. Their terrarium-building workshops come highly recommended.

PARKS AND SWIMMING

Dublin is no concrete jungle. Dotted with green spaces, Dublin is even home to Europe's largest city park, providing plenty of places to relax and unwind. And with Dublin located right at the sea, there are also lots of spots to go swimming. The water may never reach Mediterranean temperatures, but that doesn't stop the Irish from diving in. Make sure to check the tides and water quality on *beaches.ie* before taking a dip yourself. Here's a list of just a few of the city's best parks, gardens, and swimming spots.

St. Stephen's Green

Still in its original Victorian layout, St. Stephen's Green is Dublin's most famous park, located right in the heart of the city. Just steps from the busy shopping streets of South Dublin, it offers a peaceful retreat. The park has played a key role in the city's history and is home to fifteen monuments commemorating Irish heritage. It also features a floral garden, a lake, a playground, and a garden for the visually impaired. It is closed after dark.

St. Stephen's Green, City Centre, Dublin 2, ststephensgreenpark.ie

Merrion Square Park

One of Dublin's grandest Georgian squares, Merrion Square was once home to many rich and famous residents like W.B. Yeats and Oscar Wilde (look for plaques on the houses). The park, restored to its original layout, features tree-lined paths, colourful flower beds, and a statue of Wilde reclining on a rock. On Sundays, artists sell their works along the railings. Closed after dark.

1 Merrion Square East, South-East Inner City, Dublin 2

Herbert Park

This park in Ballsbridge was gifted to the city in 1903 by the 14th Earl of Pembroke and hosted the 1907 World Fair, of which the duck pond and bandstand still remain. Today, it offers sports courts, a playground, and a lovely Sunday food market. Closed after dark.

Herbert Park, Ballsbridge, Dublin 4

St. Anne's Park

Once home to the Guinness family, St. Anne's Estate now offers 112 hectares of parkland with many sports pitches, tennis and boules courts, a golf course, a playground, a café, and a Saturday farmers' market. Its beautiful rose garden hosts the annual Rose Festival, and you'll find Dollymount Strand, a coastal bird sanctuary, nearby.

Clontarf East, Raheny, Dublin 5

Phoenix Park

Originally a royal hunting park in the 1660s, Phoenix Park has been open to the public since 1747. A large herd of wild deer remains in the park to this day. As the largest enclosed city park in Europe, it offers plenty to explore, including Dublin Zoo, Victorian flower gardens, a café, and much more. Open 24/7.

Phoenix Park, Dublin 8, phoenixpark.ie

Bull Wall

Built in the 1800s to prevent Dublin Bay and Port from silting up, the Bull Wall is now home to the popular Bull Wall swimming shelters. With views of the iconic Poolbeg chimneys and the Happy Out café nearby for a warm drink after your swim, it's a favourite spot for a refreshing dip.

Bull Island, County Dublin

Seapoint Beach

Seapoint is a classic swimming spot that's been loved by locals and visitors for decades, with regulars taking a dip year-round. It sits right beside the historic Seapoint Martello Tower, once built to guard against invaders and now a well-known landmark. It's easy to reach by car, bus, or DART.

Seapoint, County Dublin

Forty Foot

One of Ireland's most iconic swim spots, the Forty Foot has been popular since the 19th century and famously features in James Joyce's *Ulysses* as well as the series *Bad Sisters*. Locals go swimming here year-round, with the beloved Christmas Day swim being a long-standing tradition.

Sandycove Point, Dún Laoghaire, County Dublin

Vico Bathing Place

The Vico Bathing Place has been a favourite Dublin swim spot since Vico Road was developed in the late 1800s, with regulars taking to the water year-round. It also features an adjacent seawater pool, perfect for days when the sea is too rough.

Hawk Cliff, Vico Road, Dalkey Commons, Killiney, County Dublin

HIKES & WALKS
IN DUBLIN

Howth Cliff Walk

This stunning cliff walk begins in the charming harbour village of Howth. The 7.8 km loop takes about two hours to complete and includes some steep climbs, but the breathtaking views make it all worthwhile. Along the way, you'll enjoy sweeping views of the sea, Dublin Bay, and the iconic Baily Lighthouse. Howth is easily accessible by DART, making it a perfect escape from the city.

Poolbeg Lighthouse Walk

Also known as the Great South Wall Walk, this nearly 5-kilometre seawall was completed in 1731 and was once the longest of its kind in the world. Today, it leads to the iconic red Poolbeg Lighthouse, with two main routes to choose from. The longer out-and-back route begins at Sandymount Strand, covers about 11.5 km in total, and takes you past the landmark Poolbeg chimneys. The shorter option starts at Pigeon House Road and takes around 50 to 60 minutes to complete.

Grand Canal Walkway

Starting from Grand Canal Dock in Dublin, you can follow the canal on foot as it winds out of the city and into Ireland's lush countryside. The full trail is a gentle, linear 134 km route that ends in Shannon Harbour — a journey that takes around five days to complete. Of course, you can also tackle shorter sections at your own pace. Along the way, you'll pass charming villages, centuries-old canal locks, and beautiful, ever-changing green scenery.

AROUND DUBLIN

Carrickgollogan Lead Mines Trail

This easy 1.24 mile (2 km) hike mixes history and scenery. Along the way, you'll discover fascinating landmarks such as a distinctive chimney with an external spiral staircase – a relic from mining operations active until 1913 – as well as the ruins of a church and a classic round tower. And there are sweeping views over Dublin Bay to enjoy. The trail is just a 20-minute drive from the city.

Brayhead Walk

With spectacular views over the Irish Sea and the Wicklow Mountains, this hill climb to the stone Bray Head cross on top is well worth the effort. There are two main routes: the Bray Head out-and-back trail, which takes about an hour, and a slightly longer loop that takes around 1.5 hours to complete. Bray is easily accessible by DART, with plenty of dining options in the village.

Killiney Hill Walk

Killiney Park is, yes – near the village of Killiney, just south of Dublin. Take the DART to Dalkey and stroll towards Vico Road to reach the park. There are two main hill walks: a short, direct climb to the summit of Dalkey Hill, where you'll be rewarded with spectacular views of the beach, the Wicklow Mountains, and Dublin city. The longer route forms a scenic loop through the park for those looking to stretch their legs a bit more.

The Hellfire Club Walk

This manageable walk on the southwest side of Dublin blends history with scenic views. The 2.6 mile (4,2 km) loop takes you past the ruins of the Hellfire Club on Montpelier Hill, offering sweeping views over Dublin and the surrounding countryside. According to legend, the devil once made an appearance here. The building was constructed in 1725 as a shooting lodge for the Speaker of the Irish Parliament. As public transport doesn't reach the beginning of the walk, it's best to travel by taxi from the nearest bus stop or take the entire journey by car.

VEGETARIAN AND VEGAN DUBLIN

Govinda's

One of Dublin's oldest veggie spots, Govinda's serves tasty Indian-inspired dishes at affordable prices. Known for generous portions and a relaxed atmosphere, it's a popular spot for healthy, satisfying food.

83 Middle Abbey Street, North City, Dublin 1, insta @govindas.dublin

The Saucy Cow

You don't have to be vegan to crave these burgers. Hidden down an alley in Temple Bar, this laid-back, industrial-style spot serves vegan junk food, like juicy burgers, loaded fries, and crispy hash browns that always hit the spot.

19 Crane Lane, Temple Bar, Dublin 2, thesaucycow.com

It's a Trap

Best known for their mouth-watering cinnamon rolls, this plant-based micro bakery offers plenty more delicious treats, from fresh wraps and sandwiches to gooey-filled cookies, all fully vegan.

81 Aungier Street, CIty Centre, Dublin 2, itsatrap.ie

Glas

Glas is Dublin's top vegetarian fine-dining restaurant. Their creative and delicious menu, crafted by award-winning chefs, is made with seasonal vegetables and locally sourced ingredients. Glas is also Dublin's first fully gluten-free fine dining restaurant.

15/16 Chatham Street, City Centre, Dublin 2, glasrestaurant.ie

Sprout & co.

Sprout is a locally sourced seasonal food spot that puts flavour first. With locations across the city, it's perfect for a quick but nourishing lunch. Choose from fresh bowls, salads, and wraps. While their menu is not fully vegetarian, it offers plenty of great options – or you can build your own!

19 Exchequer Street, Creative Quarter, Dublin 2, sproutfoodco.com

Umi Falafel

Branches of Umi have spread all over Ireland, but their authentic falafel is still handmade with care. Everything is freshly prepared, from the warm breads to the salads, pickles, and sauces that are made using traditional family recipes.

George's Street Arcade, Creative Quarter, Dublin 2, umifalafel.ie

Tiller + Grain

If you're a fan of fresh, sustainable, and locally sourced produce – and love vibrant salads and delicious cakes – Tiller + Grain is your kind of place. With a menu crafted by an Ottolenghi-trained chef, this bright and modern lunch spot offers creative vegetarian and vegan salads, with optional additions of fish or meat. Perfect for both plant-based eaters as well as those who aren't.

23 Frederick Street South, South-East Inner City, Dublin 2, tillerandgrain.ie

Dosa Dosa

Indian cuisine is celebrated for its flavourful vegetarian dishes, and Dosa Dosa delivers just that. On the menu: *crispy dosas* (obviously!), *uttapams*, and *kathi rolls*, all inspired by Tamil flavours. They're served with warm *sambar* (spiced lentil soup) and coconut chutney, and are best enjoyed with a refreshing mango *lassi* to round out the meal.

The Place Proper Street Food, Grand Canal Street Lower, Docklands, Dublin 2, dosadosa.ie

The Mushroom Butcher

This chef couldn't find high-quality mushrooms in Ireland and started growing them in a 50m2 Dublin townhouse. He now delivers to Michelin-starred restaurants, and on Saturdays caters to his loyal clientele from his food truck. Expect wraps filled with gourmet mushrooms, and even sweet and savoury doughnuts.

90 South Circular Road, Portobello, Dublin 8, insta @mushroombutcher

The Happy Pear

Technically just outside Dublin, the world-famous Happy Pear still earns its place on this list. It is known for vibrant, whole-food, plant-based dishes. Run by the energetic Flynn twins – because it takes a pair to run The Happy Pear.

Church Road, Rathdown Lower, Greystones, County Wicklow, thehappypear.ie

OUTSIDE OF DUBLIN

Boyne Valley

5,000 years of Irish history – all in one valley. Prehistoric times come to life in UNESCO world heritage Brú na Bóinne. The high kings of Ireland ruled from the top of the Hill of Tara and the Hill of Ward. The Anglo-Normans built Trim Castle and Slane Castle. In the 5th century, early Christian monks created the monastery Monasterboice. Mellifont Abbey followed in the 12th century. And the good news is that it's all still there!
But the valley offers more than just a few slices of history. It has been recognised as one of the world's best food destinations. Local produce is of high quality and a great inspiration for local chefs, cheesemongers, and distillers alike. Take a 40-minute drive from Dublin city centre or take the train from Connolly Station to Drogheda and bus 163 to Brú na Bóinne.

Cooley Peninsula

This peninsula close to Northern Ireland has a mind-boggling geology: its sandstones are 440 million years old, its limestones 340 million years, and its volcanic rocks 60 million years. And its diversity goes beyond its geology. From peaks to sandy beaches to loughs, from ancient portal stones to Ireland's prettiest villages – all packed into Cooley Peninsula's 155 square kilometres. Take the car or go hiking and cycling. From Dublin, it's a 1.5-hour drive.

County Kildare

With three rivers running through it, County Kildare is known for its lush landscapes and beautiful gardens. Its real claim to fame, however, is the horse – and not your average galloper or trotter. At the Irish National Stud, world-class racehorses are bred, and many stars have been born. Around the county, horse races abound, so be sure to go along for the ride. A visit to Ireland's first and largest Palladian mansion, Castletown House and Parklands, completes the posh experience. Kildare Village is a 40-minute drive, or a 50-minute train ride from Heuston Station.

Kilkenny

Longtime home to a famous brewery, Kilkenny is not only known for the beer named after it but also for its historic buildings. Walk Ireland's Medieval Mile and visit Kilkenny Castle and St. Canice's Cathedral, both dating back to the 13th century. The Celtic-Christian round tower next to the cathedral is even four centuries older. You can take a Dublin Coach from the city centre or a train from Dublin Heuston, both options take around 1.5 hours.

Killiney

It wasn't until the 1960s that this longtime rural village started to grow into the wealthy south-of-Dublin suburb it is today. This is where some of Ireland's richest and most famous reside. But don't go celebrity-hunting and immerse yourself in the outdoors instead: climb Killiney Hill, take a swim in Killiney Bay, wander Sorrento Park and bathe in the secluded Vico Baths. About 30 minutes by DART from the city centre.

Malahide

Malahide is the other celebrity outpost of Dublin. The Vikings landed north of what is now Dublin Bay in 795 and used it as their base for almost 400 years. When the Anglo-Normans arrived, the area was subsequently given to the Talbot family by King Henry II. The Talbots built Malahide Castle, which they occupied until 1976. The castle and its extensive gardens are now open to the public. About 30 minutes by DART from the city centre.

Skerries

Named after the five rocky islands before its shore, Skerries is a lovely coastal town and fishing port. Go there for the obvious: sandy beaches, kayaking, paddling, and seafood restaurants. However, don't forget the less obvious: defensive towers, castles, and windmills. Altogether, they make for an exciting day trip north of Dublin. 50 Minutes by train from Connolly Station.

Wicklow Mountains National Park

Close to Dublin, yet of a completely different nature. Experience Ireland's ancient wilderness in the largest of its eight national parks. Nine trails take you over its mountains, through its woods, down to its hidden lakes, and along its raging streams. Admire the biodiversity and different views and landscapes and marvel at the remains of St. Kevin's monastery in Glendalough. Depending on your destination, it's 1 to 1.5 hours by car.

↓ KILKENNY

INDEX

Neighbourhoods 8
Practical info 12
Travel 14
Where to stay 20
Good to know 24
When to travel 30
Life in Dublin 40
History 42
Sightseeing 52 (see below)
Museums 58 (see below)
Street art 66
Cinema & theatres 70
Festivals 72
Dublin Tours 74
Things to do 78
Famous people 82
Films & series in and about Dublin 86
Books in & about Dublin 90
Fun Facts 96
Photo Spots 100 (see below)
Food and Drinks 106 (see below)
Going Out 130 (see below)
Shopping 144 (see below)
Green Dublin 170
Parks and swimming 172
Hikes 177
Vegetarian and vegan Dublin 180 (see below)
Outside of Dublin 184 (see below)

SIGHTSEEING 50

Christ Church Cathedral 55
Dublin Castle 53
Four Courts, The 54
Garden of Remembrance, The 52
Georgian squares 52
National Botanic Gardens 55
National Library of Ireland, The 53
Old Library of Trinity College Dublin 53
Saint Patrick's Cathedral 54

MUSEUMS 58

Chester Beatty 60
EPIC 58
14 Henrietta Street 58
Hugh Lane Gallery 59
IMMA 64
Kilmainham Gaol Museum 64
Little Museum of Dublin, The 60
Museum of Literature Ireland 60
National Gallery of Ireland 61
National Museum of Ireland 64
Photo Museum Ireland 61

PHOTO SPOTS 100

Dublin Bay 104
Dublin Doors 100
Grand Canal Docks 104
Ha'Penny Bridge 100
Oscar Wilde Memorial 105
Samuel Beckett Bridge 105
Spire, The 103
Sunrise over Dublin Bay 104
Synod Hall Bridge 103
Temple Bar Pub, The 103
Trinity College Dublin 104

FOOD AND DRINKS 106

3fe 108
Airfield Farmers' Market 113
Alma 109
Bakeries 110
Bambino 116
Bar Pez 122
Beshoff Bros 119
Bibi's Café 109
BIGFAN 123
Bread 41 110
Breakfast, brunch & coffee 108
Brew Lab 108
Bring the parents 129

Brother Hubbard 108
Bunsen 123
Chimac 123
Cookieboy 114
Darkey Kelly's 121
DiFontaine's 116
Doom Slice 116
Dún Laoghaire CoCo Market 113
El Silencio Fff 123
Elliot's 112
Fable Bakery 112
Fambally 112, The
Fish & Chips 116
Fish Shop 119
Groundstate Coffee Roasters 109
Grove Road 109
Hang Dai 124
Hath Coffee 110
Hera 129
Herbert Park Farmers' Market 113
Irish Village Markets 114
Juice Yard 110
Kaph 108
Kyoto Asian Street Food 128
Leo Burdock 119
Lincoln's Inn 121
Little Forest 128
Loose Canon 121
Lunch & Dinner 122
Mama's Revenge 124
Mani 116
Masa 124
Mind the Step 108
Murphy's Ice Cream 114
Nomo ramen 124
O'Neill's 119
Octopussy's Seafood Tapas 128
Place Proper Street Food, The 112
Pub Grub 119
Rolling Donut, The 114
Russel Street bakery 110
Scoop Dessert Parlour 114
September 129
Shouk 128
Slices 116

Space Jaru 128
Spitalfields 129
Split Milk 116
St. Anne's Park Market 113
Street food & Farmers' Markets 112
Suertudo 129
Sweet Tooth 114
Tang 123
Two Faced 121
Two Pups Coffee 110
Una Bakery 112
Vice Pizza & Wing Shop 124
Wine Bars 121
Xi'an Street Food 122

GOING OUT 130

4 Dame Lane 139
Bad Bobs 139
Bar with No Name, The 137
Beer Bars 137
Bernard Shaw, The 136
Bonobo 138
BrewDowg Dublin Outpost 137
Club & Pub-Clubs 138
Copper Face Jacks 140
Dicey's Garden 140
Fagan's 136
Fidelity Bar 138
George, The 140
Grand Social, The 138
Hill, The 133
Hogan's Bar 140
Hole in The Wall, The 133
Izakaya Basement 139
John Kavanagh The Gravediggers 137
Kehoes 132
Kodiak 137
Mother Club 140
O'Donohue's 133
O'Reagan's 133
Old Stand, The 132
Palace Bar, The 132
PantiBar 140
Pubs 132

Queer
Rag Trader, The 132
Stag's Head, The 132
Wigwam 139
Workman's Club, The 139

SHOPPING 144
How to dress like a local 146
Affordable Art & Home Deco 166
Antiques 152
Art & Craft Supplies 162
Bookshops 158
Fashion & Department Stores 156
Flea Markets 151
Made in Ireland 164
Shops We Love 168
Streetwear 154
Vintage 148
Vinyl & CDs 166

GREEN DUBLIN 170
Parks and swimming 172
Hikes & walks in Dublin 177
Hikes & walks around Dublin 178

VEGETARIAN AND VEGAN DUBLIN 180
Dosa Dosa 183
Glas 181
Govinda's 181
Happy Pear, The 183
It's a trap 181
Mushroom Butcher, The 183
Saucy Cow, The 181
Sprout & co. 182
Tiller + Grain 182
Umi Falafel 182

OUTSIDE OF DUBLIN 184
Boyne Valley 184
Cooley Peninsula 184
County Kildare 185
Kilkenny 185
Killiney 186
Malahide 186
Skerries 186
Wiclow Mountains National Park 187

ABOUT THE AUTHOR

Flo Schreinemachers

Flo Schreinemachers is a Dutch architecture student who spent part of her studies at UCD in Dublin and returns to the city whenever she can. When in Dublin, she fully embraces the city's lifestyle – from plunging into the icy waters of Dublin Bay to hiking with friends in the lush green surroundings, and ending the day in one of its iconic pubs. As a student and true food lover, Flo is always on the lookout for the latest trendy and affordable spots, while also seeking out hidden gems that most visitors miss. With a deep appreciation for Dublin's rich history and traditional pub culture, she sees the city as the perfect blend of old and new – a place where there's always something new to discover.

WHY SHOULD I GO TO DUBLIN
the city you definitely need to visit
before you turn 30 (or 130)

Concept
mo'media

Text and address selection
Flo Schreinemachers

Art direction and illustration design
Jelle F. Post

Editing
Ezra van Wilgenburg, Maaike van Steekelenburg

Photography
Tal Maes, Rosa Schreinemachers

Published in 2025 by
mo'media Rotterdam,
The Netherlands, momedia.nl

All rights reserved. No part of this publication may be copied, displayed, extracted, reproduced, utilised, stored in a retrieval system or transmitted in any form or by any means, electronic, mechanical or otherwise including but not limited to photocopying, recording, or scanning without the prior written permission of the publisher.

(m) Copyright © mo'media BV, 2025

Why Should I Go To Dublin
ISBN 978 94 9333 872 2
NUR 510

Disclaimer
The points of interested mentioned in this travel guide have been selected by the author. None of them have been paid for inclusion in this book: the *Why Should I Go To* book series is entirely ad-free.

Publisher's Note
Every effort has been made to ensure that the information in this book is accurate at the time of going to press. The publisher welcomes any information or suggestions for correction or improvement. Please send us an e-mail at info@momedia.nl.

 whyshouldigoto

WHY SHOULD I GO TO?
Information on all our travel guides
on **WHYSHOULDIGOTO.COM**

Why Should I Go To travel guides are available for the following cities: Amsterdam, Antwerp, Barcelona, Berlin, Budapest, Copenhagen, Dublin, Lisbon, London, Paris, Prague, Rome, Rotterdam and Valencia. More cities will be added soon.